VISUAL QUICKSTART GUIDE

PYTHON

Second Edition

Toby Donaldson

Peachpit Press

Visual QuickStart Guide
Python, Second Edition
Toby Donaldson

Peachpit Press
1249 Eighth Street
Berkeley, CA 94710
510/524-2178
510/524-2221 (fax)

Find us on the Web at www.peachpit.com.
To report errors, please send a note to errata@peachpit.com.
Peachpit Press is a division of Pearson Education.

Editors: Clifford Colby and Elissa Rabellino
Production Editor: Myrna Vladic
Compositor: Debbie Roberti
Indexer: Julie Bess
Cover Design: Peachpit Press

ISBN 13: 978-0-321-58544-8
ISBN 10: 0-321-58544-5

9 8 7 6 5 4 3 2 1

Printed and bound in the United States of America

Acknowledgments

Thanks to Clifford Colby and Elissa Rabellino, for their expertise and patience in bringing this book to life; to the many students at SFU who continue to teach me how best to learn Python; to John Edgar and the other computer science teachers at SFU with whom I've had the pleasure to work; to Bonnie, for her wise advice to avoid using the word *blithering* more than once in these acknowledgments; and to Thomas, for resisting the at-times clearly overwhelming urge to eat, tear, or suck on early drafts of this book.

And a special thank-you to Guido van Rossum and the rest of the Python community, for creating a programming language that is so much fun to use.

TABLE OF CONTENTS

TABLE OF CONTENTS

Introduction
to Programming

Before we dive into the details of Python programming, it helps to learn a bit about what Python is and what kinds of programs it is used for. We will also outline exactly what it is that programmers do. Finally, we'll learn how to install Python and run the IDLE editor that comes with it.

If you are new to programming, this short introduction should help you get your footing in preparation for learning the Python programming language.

If you already have a grasp of the basic concepts, feel free to jump ahead to the sections on how to install Python and run the editor.

The Python Language

So what is Python? Briefly, it is a computer *programming language* and a corresponding set of software tools and libraries. It was originally developed in the early 1990s by Guido van Rossum, and it is now actively maintained by dozens of programmers around the world (including van Rossum).

Python was designed to be easy to read and learn. Compared with programs written in most other programming languages, Python programs look neat and clean: Python has few unnecessary symbols, and it uses straightforward English names instead of the cryptic syntax common in other languages (Ruby and Perl, I'm looking at you!).

Python is a very productive language: Once you're proficient with Python, you can get more done with it in less time than you can in most other programming languages. Python supports—but doesn't force you to use—*object-oriented programming* (OOP).

Python comes with a wide range of ready-made libraries that can be (freely!) used in your own programs; as some Python programmers like to say, Python comes with "batteries included."

One of the most important features of Python is its *maintainability*: Since Python programs are relatively easy to read and modify, they are easy for programmers to keep up to date. Program maintenance can easily account for 50 percent or more of the work a programmer does, and so Python's support for maintenance is a big win in the eyes of many professionals.

Finally, a word about the name. According to Python's originator, Guido van Rossum, Python was named after the Monty Python comedy troupe. Despite this mirthful origin, Python now uses a pair of iconic blue and yellow snakes—presumably pythons—as its standard symbol.

What Is Python Useful For?

While Python is a general-purpose language that can be used to write any kind of program, it is especially popular for the following applications:

◆ **Scripts.** These short programs automate common administrative tasks, such as adding new users to a system, uploading files to a Web site, downloading Web pages without using a browser, and so on. Due to its simplicity, Python is also a popular choice as a scripting language for many products, such as the video game Civilization 4.

◆ **Web-site development.** A number of Python projects—such as Django (www.djangoproject.com), Turbo Gears (www.turbogears.org), and Zope (www.zope.org)—are popular among many Web-site developers as tools for quickly creating dynamic Web sites. For instance, the popular news site www.reddit.com was written using Python.

◆ **Text processing.** Python has excellent support for handling strings and text files, including regular expressions and Unicode.

◆ **Scientific computing.** Many superb scientific Python libraries are available on the Web, providing functions for statistics, mathematics, and graphing.

◆ **Education.** Thanks to its relative simplicity and utility, Python is becoming more and more popular as a first programming language in schools.

Of course, Python isn't the best choice for all kinds of programming projects. Python is often less efficient than languages such as Java, C, and C++. So, for example, you wouldn't use Python to create a new operating system.

But when you need to minimize the amount of time a *programmer* spends on a project, Python is often an excellent choice.

How Programmers Work

While there is no recipe for writing programs, it is helpful to understand the basic steps that all programmers follow.

The programming process

1. Determine what your program is supposed to do—that is, figure out its *requirements*.

2. Write the source code (in our case, the Python code) in IDLE (short for Python's Integrated Development Environment) or any other text editor. Python source code files end with *.py*: web.py, urlexpand.py, clean.py, and so on. This is often the most interesting and challenging step, and it often involves creative problem solving.

3. Convert the source code to *object code* using the Python *interpreter*. Python puts object code in .pyc files. For example, if your source code is in urlexpand.py, its object code will be put in urlexpand.pyc.

4. *Run*, or *execute*, the program. With Python, this step is usually done immediately and automatically after step 2 is finished. Thus, in practice, Python programmers rarely work directly with object code or .pyc files.

5. Finally, *check* the program's output. If errors are discovered, go back to step 1 to try to fix them. The process of fixing errors is called *debugging*. For large or complex programs, debugging can sometimes take up most of the program development time, so experienced programmers try to design their programs in ways that will minimize debugging time.

As **Figure 1.1** shows, this is an *iterative* process: You write your program, test it, fix errors, test it again, and so on until the program behaves correctly.

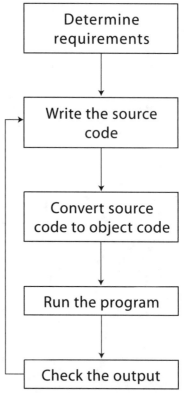

Figure 1.1 The basic steps of writing any computer program. Typically, after you check your program output, you find errors and so must go back to the code-writing step to fix them.

Lingo Alert

We typically call the contents of a .py file a *program*, *source code*, or just *code*.

Object code is sometimes referred to as *executable code*, the *executable*, or even just *software*.

Figure 1.2 The starting screen of the IDLE editor. The first line tells you which version of Python you are using—in this case, it's version 3.0b1.

Installing Python

Python is a hands-on language, so now we will see how to install it on your computer.

To install Python on Windows:

1. Go to the Python download page at www.python.org/download using your favorite Web browser.

2. Choose the most recent version of Python 3 (it should have a name like Python 3.x, where x is some small number). This will take you to the appropriate download page with instructions for downloading Python on different computer systems.

3. Click the appropriate installer link for your computer. For instance, if you are running Windows, click Windows x86 MSI Installer (3.x).

4. Once the installer has finished downloading, run it by double-clicking it.

5. After the installation has finished (which could take a few minutes), test to see that Python is installed properly. Open the Windows Start menu and choose All Programs. You should see an entry for Python 3.0 (often highlighted in yellow). Select IDLE (Python GUI), and wait a moment for the IDLE program to launch (**Figure 1.2**).

6. Try typing in *24 * 7* and pressing Return. The number 168 should appear.

INSTALLING PYTHON

Installing Python on the Mac

Mac OS X already comes with a version of Python installed, although it is typically not the most up-to-date version and lacks the IDLE editor. To install a more recent version of Python, follow the instructions given at www.python.org/download/mac/. Or, just download and run an installer from www.pythonmac.org/packages/. Be careful to ensure that you have the right version of Python (3.0 or better) and that the Mac OS X version number matches yours.

Installing Python on Linux

If you are using Linux, chances are you already have Python installed. To find out, open a command-line window and type *python*. If you get something similar to the text shown in Figure 1.2, then you have Python.

Be sure to check the version number: This book covers Python 3. If you have Python 2.x or earlier, then you should install Python 3.

The exact details for doing so will depend upon your Linux system. For example, on Ubuntu Linux, you would search for Python in the Synaptic Package Manager. You can also get Linux installation help from www.python.org/download.

ARITHMETIC, STRINGS, AND VARIABLES

The first step in learning how to program is to understand the basic Python *data types*: integers (whole numbers), floating point numbers (numbers with a decimal point), and strings. All programs use these (and other) data types, so it is important to have a good grasp of their basic uses.

Strings, in particular, are used in so many different kinds of programs that Python provides a tremendous amount of support for them. In this chapter, we'll just introduce the bare basics of strings, and then we'll return to them in a later chapter.

We'll also introduce the important concept of a programming *variable*. Variables are used to store and manipulate data, and it's hard to write a useful program without employing at least a few of them.

Just like learning how to play the piano or speak a foreign language, the best way to learn how to program is to *practice*. Thus, we'll introduce all of this using the interactive command shell IDLE, and ideally you should follow along on your own computer by typing the examples as we go.

The Interactive Command Shell

Let's see how to interact with the Python shell. Start IDLE; you should find it listed as a program in your Start menu on Windows. On Mac or Linux you should be able to run it directly from a command line by typing *python*. The window that pops up is the Python *interactive command shell*, and it looks something like what's shown in **Figure 2.1**.

The shell prompt

In a Python transcript, >>> is the Python *shell prompt*. A >>> marks a line of input from you, the user, while lines without a >>> are generated by Python. Thus it is easy to distinguish at a glance what is from Python and what is from you.

Transcripts

A *shell transcript* is a snapshot of the command shell showing a series of user inputs and Python replies. We'll be using them frequently; they're a great way to learn Python by seeing real examples in action.

Lingo Alert

The interactive command shell is often abbreviated as *interactive shell*, *command shell*, *shell*, or even *command line*.

Shell transcripts are sometimes called *transcripts*, *interactive sessions*, or just *sessions*.

```
Python 3.0b1 (r30b1:64403M, Jun 19 2008, 14:56:09) [MSC v.1500 32
bit (Intel)] on win32
Type "copyright", "credits" or "license()" for more information.


****************************************************************
Personal firewall software may warn about the connection IDLE
makes to its subprocess using this computer's internal loopback
interface. This connection is not visible on any external
interface and no data is sent to or received from the Internet.
****************************************************************

IDLE 3.0b1
>>>
```

Figure 2.1 What you should see when you first launch the Python interactive command shell. The top two lines tell you what version of Python you are running. The version you see here is Python 3.0b1, and it was created a little before 3 p.m. on Thursday, June 19, 2008 (not that the creation date matters to us!).

Integer Arithmetic

An integer is a whole number, such as 25, -86, or 0. Python supports the four basic arithmetic operations: + (addition), - (subtraction), * (multiplication), and / (division). Python also uses ** for exponentiation and % to calculate remainders (for example, 25 % 7 is 4 because 7 goes into 25 three times, with 4 left over).

For example:

```
>>> 5 + 9
14
>>> 22 - 6
16
>>> 12 * 14
168
>>> 22 / 7
3.1428571428571428
>>> 2 ** 4
16
>>> 25 % 7
4
>>> 1 + 2 * 3
7
>>> (1 + 2) * 3
9
```

Integer division

Python also has an *integer division* operator, //. It works like /, except that it always returns an integer. For example, 7 // 3 evaluates to the integer 2; the digits after the decimal are simply chopped off (// does no rounding!).

Order of evaluation

Table 2.1 summarizes Python's basic arithmetic operators. They are grouped from lowest *precedence* to highest precedence. For example, when Python evaluates the expression 1 + 2 * 3, it does * before + because * has higher precedence (so it evaluates to 7—not 9!). Operators at the same level of precedence are evaluated in the order they are written. You can use *round brackets*, ( ), to change the order of evaluation—so, for example, (1 + 2) * 3 evaluates to 9. In other words, Python arithmetic follows the same evaluation rules as regular arithmetic.

Unlimited size

Unlike most other programming languages, Python puts no limit on the size of an integer. You can do calculations involving numbers with dozens (or hundreds, or thousands) of digits:

```
>>> 27 ** 100
136891479058588375991326027382088315966463695625337436471480190078368997177499076593800206155688941388250484440597994042813512732765695774566001
```

Table 2.1

Basic Arithmetic Operators		
NAME	OPERATOR	EXAMPLE
addition	+	>>> 3 + 4 7
subtraction	-	>>> 5 - 3 2
multiplication	*	>>> 2 * 3 6
division	/	>>> 3 / 2 1.5
integer division	//	>>> 3 // 2 1
remainder	%	>>> 25 % 3 1
exponentiation	**	>>> 3 ** 3 27

```
>>> 3.8 + -43.2
-39.400000000000006
>>> 12.6 * 0.5
6.2999999999999998
>>> 12.6 + 0.01
12.609999999999999
>>> 365.0 / 12
30.416666666666668
>>> 8.8 ** -5.4
7.939507629591553e-06
>>> 5.6 // 1.2
4.0
>>> 5.6 % 3.2
2.3999999999999995
```

Figure 2.2 Examples of basic floating point arithmetic using the Python command shell. Notice that approximation errors are quite common, so exact values are rarely printed.

Floating Point Arithmetic

Floating point arithmetic is done with *floating point numbers,* which in Python are numbers that contain a decimal point. For instance, -3.1, 2.999, and -4.0 are floating point numbers. We'll call them *floats* for short.

All the basic arithmetic operations that work with integers also work with floats, even **%** (remainder) and **//** (integer division). See **Figure 2.2** for some examples.

Float literals

Very large or small floats are often written in *scientific notation:*

```
>>> 8.8 ** -5.4
7.939507629591553e-06
```

The **e-06** means to multiply the preceding number by 10^{-6}. You can use scientific notation directly if you like:

```
>>> 2.3e02
230.0
```

Python is quite forgiving about the use of decimal points:

```
>>> 3.
3.0
>>> 3.0
3.0
```

You can write numbers like 0.5 with or without the leading 0:

```
>>> .5
0.5
>>> 0.5
0.5
```

✔ Tips

■ It's usually clearer to write **5.0** instead of **5.**, as the latter notation can be quite confusing—it looks like the end of a sentence.

■ The difference between **5** and **5.0** matters: **5** is an integer, while **5.0** is a floating point number. Their internal representations are significantly different.

Overflow

Unlike integers, floating point numbers have minimum and maximum values that, if exceeded, will cause *overflow errors*. An overflow error means you've tried to calculate a number that Python cannot represent as a float, because it is either too big or too small (**Figure 2.3**). Overflow errors can be *silent errors*, meaning that Python may just do the calculation incorrectly without telling you that anything bad has happened. Generally speaking, it is up to you, the programmer, to avoid overflow errors.

Limited precision

Precision (that is, accuracy) is a fundamental difficulty with floats on all computers. Numbers are represented in binary (base 2) in a computer, and it turns out that not all floating point numbers can be represented precisely in binary. Even the simplest examples can have problems:

```
>>> 1 / 3
0.33333333333333331
```

This should have an infinite number of 3s after the decimal, but there are only (!) 17 digits here. Plus, the last digit is wrong (the 1 should be a 3).

```
>>> 500.0 ** 10000
Traceback (most recent call last):
    File "<pyshell#38>", line 1, in
    → <module>
        500.0 ** 10000
OverflowError: (34, 'Result too large')
```

Figure 2.3 Floating point overflow: Python cannot store the result of 500.0 ** 10000 as a float.

These small errors are not usually a problem: 17 digits after the decimal is enough for most programs. However, little errors have a nasty habit of becoming big errors when you are doing lots of calculations. If you are, say, computing the stresses on a newly designed bridge, it is necessary to take these floating point approximations into account to ensure that they don't balloon into significant errors.

✔ Tip

- In general, you should prefer integers to floating point numbers. They are always accurate and never suffer overflow.

Complex numbers

Python has built-in support for complex numbers—that is, numbers that involve the square root of -1. In Python, `1j` denotes the square root of -1:

```
>>> 1j
1j
>>> 1j * 1j
(-1+0j)
```

Complex numbers are useful in certain engineering and scientific calculations; we won't be using them again in this book.

FLOATING POINT ARITHMETIC

Other Math Functions

Python comes with many different *modules* of prewritten code, including the `math` module. **Table 2.2** lists some of the most commonly used `math` module functions.

Using return values

We say that these functions *return* a value. That means they *evaluate* to either an integer or a floating point number, depending on the function.

You can use these functions anywhere that you can use a number. Python automatically evaluates the function and replaces it with its return value.

Importing a module

To use the `math` module, or any existing Python module, you must first *import* it:

```
>>> import math
```

You can now access any math function by putting `math.` in front of it:

```
>>> math.sqrt(5)
2.2360679774997898
>>> math.sqrt(2) * math.tan(22)
0.012518132023611912
```

An alternative way of importing a module is this:

```
>>> from math import *
```

Now you can call all the math module functions *without* first appending `math.`:

```
>>> log(25 + 5)
3.4011973816621555
>>> sqrt(4) * sqrt(10 * 10)
20.0
```

Table 2.2

Some math Module Functions

NAME	DESCRIPTION
ceil(x)	Ceiling of x
cos(x)	Cosine of x
degrees(x)	Converts x from radians to degrees
exp(x)	e to the power of x
factorial(n)	Calculates n! = 1*2*3*...*n n must be an integer
log(x)	Base e logarithm of x
log(x, b)	Base b logarithm of x
pow(x, y)	x to the power of y
radians(x	Converts x from degrees to radians
sin(x)	Sine of x
sqrt(x)	Square root of x
tan(x)	Tangent of x

✔ Tips

■ When using the `from math import *` style of importing, if you have functions with the same name as any of the functions in the `math` module, the `math` functions will overwrite them!

■ Thus, it's generally *safer* to use the `import math` style of importing. This will never overwrite existing functions.

■ You can also import specific functions from the `math` module. For example, `from math import sqrt, tan` imports just the `sqrt` and `tan` functions.

Strings

A string is a sequence of one or more characters, such as `"cat!"`, `"567-45442"`, and `"Up and Down"`. Characters include letters, numbers, punctuation, plus hundreds of other special symbols and unprintable characters.

Indicating a string

Python lets you indicate *string literals* in three main ways:

◆ Single quotes, such as `'http'`, `'open house'`, or `'cat'`

◆ Double quotes, such as `"http"`, `"open house"`, or `"cat"`

◆ Triple quotes, such as `"""http"""`, or multiline strings, such as

```
"""
Me and my monkey
Have something to hide
"""
```

✔ Tips

■ Many Python programmers prefer using single quotes to indicate strings, simply because they involve less typing than double quotes (which require pressing the Shift key).

■ One of the main uses of single and double quotes is to conveniently handle " and ' characters inside strings:

```
"It's great"
'She said "Yes!"'
```

■ You'll get an error if you use the wrong kind of quote within a string.

■ Triple quotes are useful when you need to create long, multiline strings. They can also contain " and ' characters at the same time.

STRINGS

String length

To determine the number of characters in a string, use the `len(s)` function:

```
>>> len('pear')
4
>>> len('up, up, and away')
16
>>> len("moose")
5
>>> len("")
0
```

The last example uses the *empty string*, usually denoted by `''` or `""`. The empty string has zero characters in it.

Since `len` evaluates to (that is, returns) an integer, we can use `len` anywhere that an integer is allowed—for example:

```
>>> 5 + len('cat') * len('dog')
14
```

String Concatenation

You can create new strings by "adding" together old strings:

```
>>> 'hot ' + 'dog'
'hot dog'
>>> 'Once' + " " + 'Upon' + ' ' +
→ "a Time"
'Once Upon a Time'
```

This operation is known as *concatenation*.

There's a neat shortcut for concatenating the same string many times:

```
>>> 10 * 'ha'
'hahahahahahahahahaha'
>>> 'hee' * 3
'heeheehee'
>>> 3 * 'hee' + 2 * "!"
'heeheehee!!'
```

The result of string concatenation is always another string, so you can use concatenation anywhere that requires a string:

```
>>> len(12 * 'pizza pie!')
120
>>> len("house" + 'boat') * '12'
'121212121212121212'
```

Getting Help

Python is a largely *self-documenting* language. Most functions and modules come with brief explanations to help you figure out how to use them without resorting to a book or Web site.

Listing functions in a module

Once you've imported a module, you can list all of its functions using the dir(m) function:

```
>>> import math
>>> dir(math)
['__doc__', '__name__', '__package__',
'acos', 'acosh', 'asin', 'asinh',
'atan', 'atan2', 'atanh', 'ceil',
'copysign', 'cos', 'cosh', 'degrees',
'e', 'exp', 'fabs', 'factorial',
'floor', 'fmod', 'frexp', 'hypot',
'isinf', 'isnan', 'ldexp', 'log',
'log10', 'log1p', 'modf', 'pi', 'pow',
'radians', 'sin', 'sinh', 'sqrt', 'sum',
'tan', 'tanh', 'trunc']
```

This gives you a quick overview of the functions in a module, and many Python programmers use dir(m) all the time.

For now, you can ignore the names beginning with a double underscore __; they are used only in more advanced Python programming.

✔ Tips

- To see a list of all the built-in functions in Python, type `dir(__builtins__)` at the command prompt.

- An alternative way to see the doc string for a function `f` is to use the `help(f)` function.

- You can run the *Python help utility* by typing `help()` at a prompt. This will provide you with all kinds of useful information, such as a list of all available modules, help with individual functions and keywords, and more.

- You can also get help from the Python documentation (www.python.org/doc/). There you'll find helpful tutorials, plus complete details of all the Python language and standard modules.

Printing documentation strings

Another useful trick is to print a function's *documentation string* (*doc string* for short):

```
>>> print(math.tanh.__doc__)
tanh(x)
Return the hyperbolic tangent of x.
```

Most built-in Python functions, along with most functions in Python's standard modules (such as `math`), have short doc strings you can access in this way.

As another example, here's the doc string for the built-in function `bin`:

```
>>> print(bin.__doc__)
bin(number) -> string
Return the binary representation of an
→ integer or long integer.
>>> bin(25)
'0b11001'
```

GETTING HELP

Converting Between Types

Converting from one type of data to another is a common task, and Python provides a number of built-in functions to make this easy.

Converting integers and strings to floats:

To convert the number 3 to a float, use the `float(x)` function:

```
>>> float(3)
3.0
```

Converting a string to a float is similar:

```
>>> float('3.2')
3.2000000000000002
>>> float('3')
3.0
```

Converting integers and floats to strings:

The `str(n)` function converts any number to a corresponding string:

```
>>> str(85)
'85'
>>> str(-9.78)
'-9.78'
```

Implicit Conversions

Sometimes Python will convert between numeric types without requiring an explicit conversion function. For example:

```
>>> 25 * 8.5
212.5
```

Here, 25 is automatically converted to 25.0, and then multiplied by 8.5. In general, when you mix integers and floats in the same expression, Python *automatically* converts the integers to floats.

Converting a float to an integer:

This is a little tricky because you must decide how to handle any digits after the decimal in your float. The `int(x)` function simply chops off extra digits, while `round(x)` does the usual kind of rounding off:

```
>>> int(8.64)
8
>>> round(8.64)
9
>>> round(8.5)
8
```

Converting strings to numbers:

This is easily done with the `int(s)` and `float(s)` functions:

```
>>> int('5')
5
>>> float('5.1')
5.0999999999999996
```

✔ Tips

■ For most applications, you should be able to handle numeric conversions using `int(x)`, `float(x)`, and `round(x)`. However, for more specific conversions, the Python `math` module has a number of functions for removing digits after decimals: `math.trunc(x)`, `math.ceil(x)`, and `math.floor(x)`.

■ The `int(s)` and `float(s)` conversions from strings to floats/integers assume that the string `s` "looks" like a Python float/integer. If not, you'll get an error message saying the conversion could not be done.

Variables and Values

Variables are one of the most important concepts in all of programming: In Python, variables *label*, or *point to*, a value.

For example:

```
>>> fruit = "cherry"
>>> fruit
'cherry'
```

Here, `fruit` is a variable name, and it points to the string value `"cherry"`. Notice that variables are *not* surrounded by quotation marks.

The line `fruit = "cherry"` is called an *assignment statement*. The = (equals sign) is called the *assignment operator* and is used to make a variable point to a value.

When Python encounters a variable, it replaces it with the value it points to. Thus:

```
>>> cost = 2.99
>>> 0.1 * cost
0.29900000000000004
>>> 1.06 * cost + 5.99
9.1594000000000015
```

Lingo Alert

Just like variables, functions, modules, and classes all have names. We refer to these names collectively as *identifiers*.

Table 2.3

Legal and Illegal Variable Names	
LEGAL	ILLEGAL
M	"m"
x1	1x
tax_rate	tax rate
taxRate	taxRate!
Else	else

```
>>> else = 25
SyntaxError: invalid syntax (<pyshell#3>,
→ line 1)
```

Figure 2.4 else is a Python keyword, so it cannot be used as a variable.

Rules for making variable names

Variable names must follow a few basic rules (see **Table 2.3** for some examples):

◆ A variable name can be of any length, although the characters in it must be either letters, numbers, or the underscore character (_). Spaces, dashes, punctuation, quotation marks, and other such characters are not allowed.

◆ The first character of a variable name *cannot* be a number; it must be a letter or an underscore character.

◆ Python is *case sensitive*—it distinguishes between uppercase and lowercase letters. Thus TAX, Tax, and tax are three completely different variable names.

◆ You cannot use Python *keywords* as variable names. For example, if, else, while, def, or, and, not, in, and is are some of Python's keywords (we'll learn what these are used for later in the book). If you try to use one as a variable, you'll get an error (**Figure 2.4**).

Assignment Statements

Assignment statements have three main parts: a *left-hand side*, an *assignment operator*, and a *right-hand side* (**Figure 2.5**). Assignment statements have two purposes: They *define* new variable names, and they make already-defined variables point to values. For instance:

```
>>> x = 5
>>> 2 * x + 1
11
>>> x = 99
```

The first assignment statement, x = 5, does double duty: It is an *initialization statement*. It tells Python that x is a variable and that it should be assigned the value 5. We can now use x anywhere an integer can be used.

The second assignment statement, x = 99, reassigns x to point to a different value. It does not create x, because x was already created by the previous assignment statement.

If you don't initialize a variable, Python complains with an error:

```
>>> 2 * y + 1
Traceback (most recent call last):
    File "<pyshell#6>", line 1, in
    → <module>
      2 * y + 1
NameError: name 'y' is not defined
```

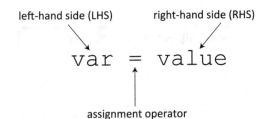

left-hand side (LHS)   right-hand side (RHS)

$$var = value$$

assignment operator

Figure 2.5 Anatomy of an assignment statement. This makes var point to value. The left-hand side must always be a variable, while the right-hand side can be a variable, value, or *any* expression that evaluates to a value.

This error message tells you that the variable y has not been defined, and so Python does not know what value to replace it with in the expression 2 * y + 1.

A variable can be assigned any value, even if it comes from other variables. Consider this sequence of assignments:

```
>>> x = 5
>>> x
5
>>> y = 'cat'
>>> y
'cat'
>>> x = y
>>> x
'cat'
>>> y
'cat'
```

Lingo Alert

A number of terms are commonly used to describe variables and values. We sometimes say a variable is *assigned* a value, or *given* a value.

A variable with an assigned value is said to *point* to its value, or *label* it, or simply *have* it.

Sometimes programmers say a variable *contains* its value, as if the variable were a bucket and the value was inside of it. The problem with this is that Python variables don't quite follow the rules you would expect a "containment" model to follow. For instance, an object can be in only one bucket at a time, but multiple values are allowed to point to the same value in Python.

How Variables Refer to Values

When Python sees an assignment statement x = expr, it treats it like the following command: *Make x point to the value that expr evaluates to.*

Keep in mind that expr can be *any* Python expression that evaluates to a value.

There's a nice way of drawing diagrams to help understand sequences of assignments. For example, after the assignment rate = 0.04, you can imagine that RAM looks like **Figure 2.6**. Then, after rate_2008 = 0.06, we get **Figure 2.7**. Finally, rate = rate_2008 gives us **Figure 2.8**.

When a value no longer has any variable pointing to it (for example, 0.04 in Figure 2.7), Python automatically deletes it. In general, Python keeps track of all values and automatically deletes them when they are no lingered referenced by a variable. This is called *garbage collection*, and so Python programmers rarely need to worry about deleting values themselves.

Figure 2.6 After running the statement rate = 0.04.

Figure 2.7 After rate_2008 = 0.06.

Figure 2.8 After rate = rate_2008. Notice that the value 0.04 no longer has any variable pointing to it. Thus Python automatically deletes it, a process known as *garbage collection*.

```
>>> s = 'apple'
>>> s + 's'
'apples'
>>> s
'apple'
>>> 5 = 1
SyntaxError: can't assign to literal
→ (<pyshell#3>, line 1)
```

Figure 2.9 Whenever it appears that you are modifying a string, Python is in fact making a copy of the string. There is no way to modify a number or a string. Thus, Python stops you from doing crazy things like setting the value of 5 to be 1.

Assignments don't copy

It's essential to understand that assignment statements *don't make a copy* of the value they point to. All they do is label, and relabel, existing values. Thus, no matter how big or complex the object a variable points to, assignment statements are always exceedingly efficient.

Numbers and strings are immutable

An important feature of Python numbers and strings is that they are *immutable*—that is, they cannot be changed in *any* way, ever. Whenever it seems that you are modifying a number or string, Python is in fact making a modified copy (**Figure 2.9**).

Multiple Assignment

Python has a convenient trick that lets you assign more than one variable at a time:

```
>>> x, y, z = 1, 'two', 3.0
>>> x
1
>>> y
'two'
>>> z
3.0
>>> x, y, z
(1, 'two', 3.0)
```

As the last statement shows, you can also display multiple values on one line by writing them as a *tuple*. Tuples always begin with an open round bracket (( ) and end with a closed round bracket ( )).

Swapping variable values

A useful trick you can do with multiple assignment is to *swap* the values of two variables:

```
>>> a, b = 5, 9
>>> a, b
(5, 9)
>>> a, b = b, a
>>> a, b
(9, 5)
```

The statement a, b = b, a is said to assign values to a and b *in parallel*. Without using multiple assignment, the standard way to swap variables is like this:

```
>>> a, b = 5, 9
>>> temp = a
>>> a = b
>>> b = temp
>>> a, b
(9, 5)
```

Multiple assignment doesn't do anything you can't already do with regular assignment. It is just a convenient shorthand that we will sometimes be using.

3

WRITING PROGRAMS

Up to now, we've been writing single Python statements and running them at the interactive command line. While that's useful for learning about Python functions, it quickly becomes tiresome when you need to solve problems that require many lines of Python code.

Thus we turn to writing *programs* (also known as *scripts*). Programs are just text files containing a collection of Python commands. When you *run* (or *execute*) a program, Python performs each statement in the file one after the other.

In this chapter, we'll learn how to write and run programs in IDLE and from the command line. We'll see how to get keyboard input from the user and print strings to the screen.

This is just the first step in writing Python programs. In the following chapters, we'll gradually explore more features for writing programs, including if statements, loops, and functions.

You should make an effort to type the code yourself, since it is an excellent way to get used to the various rules of writing Python. For larger programs, you can download the code from this book's Web site: http://pythonintro.googlecode.com.

Using IDLE's Editor

IDLE comes with a Python-aware text editor. The best way to learn about it is to write a simple program.

To write a new program in IDLE:

1. Launch IDLE.

2. Choose File > New Window.

   A blank editor window should pop up.

3. To test it, enter the following into it:

   ```
   print('Welcome to Python!')
   ```

4. Save your program by choosing File > Save. Save it in your Python programs folder with the name welcome.py; the .py at the end indicates that this is a Python file.

5. Run your program by choosing Run > Run Module.

   A Python shell should appear, and you should see *Welcome to Python!* within it.

When you start to get more familiar with the IDLE editor, you may want to start using some of the key commands listed in **Table 3.1**. They can really speed up your editing.

✔ Tips

- Create a special folder called, say, *python* on your computer's Desktop to store all your Python programs. *Never* save them in the Python directory; other-wise, you run the risk of accidentally overwriting one of Python's core files.

- You must type in Python programs *exactly* as you see them, character for character. A single wrong character—an extra space, an l instead of a 1—can cause errors.

- If you do see an error when you run your program, go back to the editor window and carefully check that your program was typed correctly, character for character.

Table 3.1

Some Useful IDLE Shortcuts

COMMAND	WHAT IT DOES
Ctrl-N	Open a new editor window.
Ctrl-O	Open a new file for editing.
Ctrl-S	Save the current program.
F5	Run the current program.
Ctrl-Z	Undo the last action.
Shift-Ctrl-Z	Redo the last undo.

Running programs from the command line

Another common way to run a Python program is from the command line. For example, to run welcome.py, you can open a command-line window and run it by typing python, followed by the filename:

```
C:\> python welcome.py
Welcome to Python!
```

To run a program from the command line:

◆ Type the following:

```
C:\> python file name.py.
```

You can also just call Python without a program and get a bare-bones (but still quite useful) version of the interactive interpreter.

To call Python from the command line:

◆ Type the following:

```
C:\> python
Python 3.0b2 (r30b2:65106, Jul 18
→ 2008, 18:44:17) [MSC v.1500 32
→ bit (Intel)] on win32
Type "help", "copyright", "credits"
→ or "license" for more information.
>>>
```

Calling Python from the command line is most commonly used when you run Python scripts as parts of other programs.

Other Editors

IDLE is an excellent editor for beginners, and even some professionals use it all the time. But if IDLE is not to your liking, you may want to try out a different programming editor, such as one of these:

◆ **Notepad2**—A fast and relatively simple Windows-only editor that has support for Python programming.

◆ **Eclipse, Emacs, Vim**—These three editors are popular with many professional programmers, and run on Windows, the Mac platform, and Linux. They have excellent support for many programming languages, Python included. However, the learning curve for any one of these editors is dauntingly steep.

Take a look at http://wiki.python.org/moin/PythonEditors for many more suggestions.

✔ Tips

■ The easiest way to open a command window in Windows is to click the Start menu; then click Run, and type cmd and press Return. This should give you a command-line window.

■ Running Python from the command line is similar on Mac and Linux systems: run a command shell (the exact details for doing this differ from system to system, but try browsing programs available through menus on your Desktop), and then type python followed by the name of the program you want to run.

■ One annoyance with running Python from the command line is that it is often necessary to configure *environment variables*, in particular your system's *path* variable, so that your system knows where to find Python on your computer. The details are finicky and system specific, and are beyond the scope of this book. However, it is not hard to find detailed instructions online if you want to set this up. For instance, just type *set windows path* into your favorite Web search engine. Take care when you are modifying environment variables: If you are not sure exactly what you are doing, it is quite possible to "break" your system so that programs no longer run correctly. In that case, your best option is usually to start over and reinstall Python.

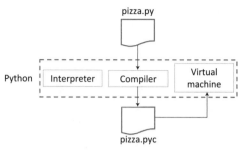

Figure 3.1 Python consists of three major components: an interpreter for running single statements; a compiler for converting .py files to .pyc files; and a virtual machine for running .pyc files. Note that IDLE is *not* strictly part of Python; it is a separate application that sits on top of Python to make it easier to use.

Compiling Source Code

We often refer to the statements inside a Python program as *source code*, and so a program file is sometimes called a *source code file*, or *source file*. By convention, all Python source code files end with the extension .py. This makes it easy for people and programs to see at a glance that the file contains Python source code.

Object code

When you run a .py file, Python automatically creates a corresponding .pyc file (**Figure 3.1**). A .pyc file contains *object code*, or *compiled code*. Object code is essentially a Python-specific language that represents your Python source code in a way that is easier for the computer to run efficiently. It is not meant for humans to read, and so most of the time you should just ignore the .pyc files that start to appear.

A Python program runs using a special piece of software called a *virtual machine*. This is essentially a software simulation of a computer designed just to run Python, and it is part of the reason why many .pyc files can run on different computer systems without any change.

✔ Tips

- You will rarely, if ever, have to worry about .pyc files. Python automatically creates them when needed, and also automatically updates them when you change the corresponding .py files. Don't delete, rename, or modify the .pyc files!

- Since they are meant to be read only by the computer, .pyc files are *not* stored as text files. If you try to view a .pyc file in a text editor, you'll see nothing but junk characters.

Reading Strings from the Keyboard

Reading a string from the keyboard is one of the most basic ways of getting information from a user. For example, consider this simple program:

```
# name.py
name = input('What is your first name? ')
print('Hello ' + name.capitalize() + '!')
```

To run this in IDLE, open name.py in an IDLE window, and then to run it press F5 (or, equivalently, choose Run > Run Module).

You should see this in the window that appears:

```
What is your first name? jack
Hello Jack!
```

You, the user, must type in the name (in this case the string 'jack').

Tracing the program

Let's look carefully at each line of the program. The first line is a *source code comment*, or *comment* for short. A comment is just a note to the programmer, and Python ignores it. Python comments always start with a # symbol and continue to the end of the line. This particular comment tells you that the program is stored in a file called name.py.

The second line calls the input function, which is the standard built-in function for reading strings from the keyboard. When it runs, the prompt 'What is your name?' appears in the output window, followed by a blinking cursor. The program waits until the user enters a string *and* presses Enter. The input function evaluates to whatever string the user enters, and so the variable name ends up labeling the string that the user types in.

The third and final line of the program displays a greeting. The function `name.capitalize()` ensures that the first character of the string is uppercase and the remaining characters are lowercase. This way, if the user happens to enter a name that isn't correctly capitalized, Python will correct it.

✔ Tips

- Don't forget to use the `dir` function to see what functions are available for strings. For example, typing `dir('')` at IDLE's interactive command line lists all of the string functions.

- If you run `name.py` with a number of sample strings, you'll soon discover that entering a name like `'Jack Aubrey'` will actually *un*capitalize the last name: `'Hello Jack aubrey!'`. That's because the `capitalize` function is very simple-minded—it knows nothing about words or spaces. Properly capitalizing a string of words requires some more advanced programming that we will see later in this book.

- Another common and useful trick when reading strings from the keyboard is to use the `strip()` function to remove any leading/trailing whitespace characters. For instance:

```
>>> ' oven '.strip()
'oven'
```

The call to `strip()` is often put directly in the input statement like this:

```
name = input('Enter age: ').strip()
```

Reading numbers from the keyboard

The `input` function only returns strings, so if you need a number data type (for example, to do arithmetic), you must use one of Python's numeric conversion functions. For example, consider this program:

```
# age.py
age = input('How old are you today? ')
age10 = int(age) + 10
print('In 10 years you will be ' +
→ str(age10) + ' years old.')
```

Suppose the user types in 22 in response to this program. Then the variable *age* labels the *string* '22'—Python does *not* automatically convert strings that look like numbers to integer or float values. If you want to do arithmetic with a string, you must first convert it to a number using either `int(s)` (if you want an integer) or `float(s)` (if you want a float).

The one final trick to notice is that in the `print` statement, it's necessary to convert the variable *age10* (which labels an integer) back into a string so that it can be printed. If you forget this conversion, Python issues an error saying it can't add numbers and strings.

Different Types of Numbers

All the different types of numbers can be confusing at first. Consider these four different values: 5, 5.0, '5', and '5.0'. While they look similar, they have very different internal representations.

5 is an integer and can be used directly for arithmetic.

5.0 is a floating point number that can also be used for arithmetic, but it allows for digits after the decimal place.

'5' and '5.0' are strings consisting of one and three characters, respectively. Strings are meant for being displayed on the screen or for doing character-based operations (such as removing whitespace or counting characters). Strings can't be used to do numeric arithmetic. Of course, strings can be used with concatenation, although the results might be a bit jarring at first—for example:

```
>>> 3 * '5'
'555'
>>> 3 * '5.0'
'5.05.05.0'
```

Printing Strings on the Screen

The `print` statement is the standard built-in function for printing strings to the screen. As we will see, it is extremely flexible and has many useful features for formatting strings and numbers in just the right way.

You can pass any number of strings to `print`:

```
>>> print('jack', 'ate', 'no', 'fat')
jack ate no fat
```

By default, it prints out each string in the *standard output* window, separating the strings with a space. You can easily change the string separator like this:

```
>>> print('jack', 'ate', 'no', 'fat',
        sep = '.')
jack.ate.no.fat
```

By default, a string ends with a *newline* character: \n. A newline character causes the cursor to move to the next line when the string is printed, and so, by default, you can't print anything on the same line after calling `print`:

```
# jack1.py
print('jack ate ')
print('no fat')
```

This prints two lines of text:

```
jack ate
no fat
```

To put all the text on a single line, you can specify the end character of the first line to be the empty string:

```
# jack2.py
print('jack ate ', end = '')
print('no fat')
```

Lingo Alert

Programmers often use the terminology *standard output*, abbreviated *stdout*, to refer to the window where text goes when printed. Typically, stdout is a simple text window that does little more than display strings: No graphics of any kind are allowed.

Similarly, *standard input*, abbreviated *stdin*, is the location from where the input function reads strings. Usually this is the same window as stdout, but it is possible to change one or both of stdout and stdin if necessary.

You will sometimes also see the term *standard error*, abbreviated *stderr*, to refer to where error messages are displayed. By default, error messages are usually displayed on stdout.

✔ Tips

- The print function is one of the major differences between Python 2 and Python 3. Before Python 3, print was not actually a function, but instead was a built-in part of the language. The one advantage of this was that you didn't have to type the brackets—for example, you would type print 'jack ate no fat'. However, despite that small convenience, print's not being a function made it very difficult to change the default separator and ending strings, which is often necessary in more advanced programs.

- Another difference between Python 2 and 3 is that Python 3's input function was called raw_input in Python 2. Python 2 also had a function called input, but it evaluated the string that the user entered, which was occasionally handy. There is no equivalent of the Python 2 input function in Python 3, although you can easily simulate it by typing eval(input(prompt)). For example:

```
>>> eval(input('? '))
? 4 + 5 * 6
34
```

Source Code Comments

We've already seen source code comments used to specify the name of a file. But comments are useful for any kind of note that you might want to put into a program, such as documentation, reminders, explanations, or warnings. Python ignores all comments, and they are only there to be read by you and other programmers who might read the source code.

Here's a sample program that shows some more uses of comments:

```python
# coins_short.py

# This program asks the user how many
# coins of various types they have,
# and then prints the total amount
# of money in pennies.

# get the number of nickels, dimes,
# and quarters from the user
n = int(input('Nickels? '))
d = int(input('Dimes? '))
q = int(input('Quarters? '))

# calculate the total amount of money
total = 5 * n + 10 * d + 25 * q

# print the results
print()  # prints a blank line
print(str(total) + ' cents')
```

Structuring a Program

As you start to write more programs, you will soon notice that they tend to follow a common structure. Typically, programs are organized as in **Figure 3.2**: They have an input part, a processing part, and an output part.

For the small programs that we are starting out with, this structure is usually obvious and does not require much thought. But as your programs get bigger and more complex, it is easy to lose sight of this overall structure, which often results in messy code that is hard to understand.

Thus, indicating in comments what parts are for input, processing, and output is a good habit to get into. It helps clarify the different tasks your program performs; and, when we start writing functions, it provides a natural way of dividing up your programs into sensible functions.

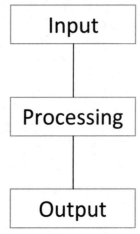

Figure 3.2 Most programs have the structure shown here: First you get input (for example, from the user using the input function), then you process it, and then you display the results for the user to see.

FLOW OF CONTROL

The programs we've written so far are *straight-line* programs that consist of a sequence of Python statements executed one after the other. The flow of execution is simply a straight sequence of statements, with no branching or looping back to previous statements.

In this chapter, we look at how to change the order in which statements are executed by using if-statements and loops. Both are essential in almost any nontrivial program.

For many beginners, if-statements and loops are two of the trickiest parts of learning how to program. Loops, in particular, can be confusing at first because they require a lot of little pieces of code to work correctly.

So take this chapter slowly and read through the sample programs carefully. Take the time to try them out and make your own modifications.

Boolean Logic

In Python, as in most programming languages, decisions are made using *Boolean logic*. In Boolean logic, there are only two *Boolean values*: True and False.

Just as with numbers and strings, you can label particular Boolean values with variables. For instance:

```
>>> front_sensor_on = True
>>> front_sensor_on
True
```

We combine Boolean values using four main *logical operators* (or *logical connectives*): not, and, or, and ==. All decisions that can be made by Python—or any computer language, for that matter—can be made using these logical operators.

Suppose that p and q are two Python variables each labeling Boolean values. Since each has two possible values (True or False), altogether there are four different sets of values for p and q (see the first two columns of **Table 4.1**). We can now define the logical operators by specifying exactly what value they return for the different truth values of p and q. These kinds of definitions are known as *truth tables*.

Table 4.1

Truth Table for Basic Logical Operators						
p	q	p == q	p != q	p and q	p or q	not p
False	False	True	False	False	False	True
False	True	False	True	False	True	True
True	False	False	True	False	True	False
True	True	True	False	True	True	False

Logical equivalence

Let's start with ==. The expression **p == q** is True just when p and q both have the same true value—that is, when p and q are both True or both False. The expression **p != q** tests if p and q are not the same, and returns True just when they have different values.

Logical "and"

The Boolean expression **p and q** is True just when both p is True and q is True. In every other case it is False. The fifth column of Table 4.1 summarizes each case.

Logical "or"

The Boolean expression **p or q** is True exactly when p is True or q is True, or when both are True. This is summarized in the sixth column of Table 4.1. It's important to realize that p or q is true when both p and q are True; Python's or is sometimes called *inclusive-or*, because it includes the case when both are True.

Logical negation

Finally, the Boolean expression **not p** is True when p is False, and False when p is True. It essentially *flips* the value of the variable.

Let's look at a few examples:

```
>>> False == False
True
>>> True and False
False
>>> False or False
False
>>> not True
False
```

Python uses an internal version of Table 4.1 to evaluate Boolean expressions.

Evaluating larger Boolean expressions

Since Boolean expressions are used to control both if-statements and loops, it is important to understand how they are evaluated. Just as with arithmetic expressions, Boolean expressions use both brackets and operator precedence to specify the order in which the subparts of the expression are evaluated.

To evaluate a Boolean expression with brackets:

◆ `not (True and (False or True))`

Expressions in brackets are always evaluated first. Thus, we first evaluate `False or True`, which is `True`, and makes the original expression equivalent to this simpler one: `not (True and True)`.

◆ `not (True and True)`

To evaluate this simpler expression, we again evaluate the expression in brackets first: `True and True` evaluates to `True`, which gives us an equivalent, but simpler, expression: `not True`.

◆ `not True`

Finally, to evaluate this expression, we simply look up the answer in the last column of Table 4.1: `not True` evaluates to `False`. Thus, the entire expression `not (True and (False or True))` evaluates to `False`. You can easily check that this is the correct answer in Python itself:

```
>>> not (True and (False or True))
False
```

Table 4.2

Boolean Operator Priority (Highest to Lowest)
p == q
p != q
not p
p and q
p or q

To evaluate a Boolean expression without brackets:

◆ `False and not False or True`

Suppose the expression you want to evaluate is this one. First evaluate the operator with the highest precedence, as listed in **Table 4.2**. In the expression `False and not False or True`, not has the highest precedence, and so `not False` is evaluated first, which causes the whole expression to simplify to `False and True or True`.

◆ `False and True or True`

In this simplified expression from the previous step, we again evaluate the operator with the highest precedence. According to Table 4.2, and has higher precedence than or, and so we evaluate `False and True` first. Thus the expression simplifies to `False or True`.

◆ `False or True`

This final expression evaluates to `True`, which is found by looking up the answer in Table 4.1. Thus the original expression, `False and not False or True`, evaluates to `True`.

✔ Tips

■ Writing complicated Boolean expressions without brackets is usually a bad idea because they are hard to read—not all programmers have the order of precedence of Boolean operators committed to memory!

■ One exception is when you use the *same* logical operator many times in a row. Then it is usually much easier to read without the brackets. For example:

```
>>> (True or (False or (True or
→ False)))
True
>>> True or False or True or False
True
```

Short-circuit evaluation

The definition of the logical operators given in Table 4.1 is the standard definition you would find in any logic textbook. However, like most modern programming languages, Python uses a technique called *short-circuit evaluation* to speed up the evaluation of some Boolean expressions.

Consider the Boolean expression False and X, where X is any Boolean expression; assume it's a big, nasty expression that would take you a few seconds to evaluate. It turns out that no matter the value of X, no matter whether X is True or X is False, the entire expression is False. The reason is that the initial False makes the whole and-expression False. In other words, the value of the expression False and X does not depend on X—it is *always* False. In such cases, Python does not evaluate X at all—it simply stops and returns the value False. This can speed up the evaluation of Boolean expressions.

Similarly, Boolean expressions of the form True or X are always True, no matter the value of X. The precise rules for how Python does short-circuiting are given in **Table 4.3**.

Most of the time you can ignore short-circuiting and just reap its performance benefits. However, it is useful to remember that Python does this, since every once in a while it could be the source of a subtle bug.

Table 4.3

Definition of Boolean Operators in Python	
OPERATION	RESULT
p or q	if p is False, then q, else p
p and q	if p is False, then p, else q

✔ Tips

- Boolean expressions of the form not X and X == Y do not do any short-circuiting: X and Y are always evaluated.

- No short-circuiting occurs in expressions of the form False or X and True or X. In both cases, X must be evaluated to determine the expression's value.

- Python applies short-circuiting inside larger Boolean expressions. So, for example, even though an entire expression might not benefit from short-circuit evaluation, some sub-expressions of it might.

- It's possible to use the definitions of and and or from Table 4.3 to write short and tricky code that simulates if-statements (which we will see in the next section). However, such expressions are usually quite difficult to read, so if you ever run across such expressions in other people's Python code (*you* should never put anything so ugly in *your* programs!), you may need to refer to Table 4.3 to figure out exactly what they are doing.

If-Statements

If-statements let you change the flow of control in a Python program. Essentially, they let you write programs that can decide, while the programming is running, whether or not to run one block of code or another. Almost all nontrivial programs use one or more if-statements, so they are important to understand.

If/else-statements

Suppose you are writing a password-checking program. You ask users to enter their password, and if it is correct, you log them in to their account. If it is not correct, then you tell them they've entered the wrong password. A simple version of that program is this:

```
# password1.py
pwd = input('What is the password? ')

if pwd == 'apple':  # note use of ==
                    # instead of =
    print('Logging on ...')
else:
    print('Incorrect password.')

print('All done!')
```

It's pretty easy to read this program: If the string that pwd labels is 'apple', then a login message is printed. But if pwd is anything other than 'apple', the message *incorrect password* is printed.

An if-statement always begins with the keyword if. It is then (always) followed by a Boolean expression called the *if-condition*, or just *condition* for short. After the if-condition comes a colon (:). As we will see, Python uses the : token to mark the end of conditions in if-statements, loops, and functions.

Everything from the `if` to the `:` is referred to as the *if-statement header*. If the condition in the header evaluates to `True`, then the statement `print('Logging on ...')` is immediately executed, and `print('Incorrect password.')` is skipped and never executed.

If the condition in the header evaluates to `False`, then `print('Logging on ...')` is skipped, and only the statement `print('Incorrect password.')` is executed.

In all cases, the final `print('All done!')` statement is executed.

The general structure of an if/else-statement is shown in **Figure 4.1**.

✔ **Tips**

■ We will often refer to the entire multiline if structure as a single if-statement.

■ You must put at least one space after the `if` keyword.

■ The `if` keyword, the condition, and the terminating `:` must appear all on one line without breaks.

■ The else-block of an if-statement is optional. Depending on the problem you are solving, you may or may not need one.

■ Python usually doesn't care about extra blank lines. Thus they are often added to group related statements together and to make the code easier for people to read.

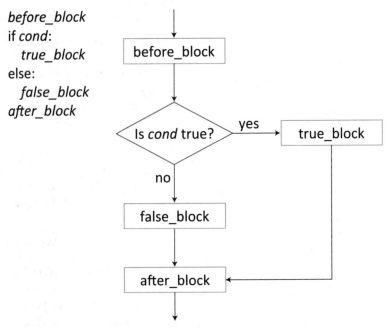

```
before_block
if cond:
    true_block
else:
    false_block
after_block
```

Figure 4.1 This flow chart shows the general format and behavior of an if/else-statement. The code blocks can consist of any number of Python statements (even other if-statements!).

Code Blocks and Indentation

One of the most distinctive features of Python is its use of indentation to mark blocks of code. Consider the if-statement from our simple password-checking program:

```python
if pwd == 'apple':
    print('Logging on ...')
else:
    print('Incorrect password.')

print('All done!')
```

The lines `print('Logging on ...')` and `print('Incorrect password.')` are two separate *code blocks*. These ones happen to be only a single line long, but Python lets you write code blocks consisting of any number of statements.

To indicate a block of code in Python, you must indent each line of the block by the same amount. The two blocks of code in our example if-statement are both indented four spaces, which is a typical amount of indentation for Python.

In most other programming languages, indentation is used only to help make the code look pretty. But in Python, it is required for indicating what block of code a statement belongs to. For instance, the final `print('All done!')` is *not* indented, and so is *not* part of the else-block.

Programmers familiar with other languages often bristle at the thought that indentation matters: Many programmers like the freedom to format their code how they please. However, Python indentation rules are quite simple, and most programmers already use indentation to make their code readable. Python simply takes this idea one step further and gives meaning to the indentation.

✔ Tips

- IDLE is designed to automatically indent code for you. For instance, pressing Return after typing the : in an if-header automatically indents the cursor on the next line.

- The amount of indentation matters: A missing or extra space in a Python block could cause an error or unexpected behavior. Statements within the same block of code need to be indented at the same level.

If/elif-statements

An if/elif-statement is a generalized if-statement with more than one condition. It is used for making complex decisions. For example, suppose an airline has the following "child" ticket rates: Kids 2 years old or younger fly for free, kids older than 2 but younger than 13 pay a discounted child fare, and anyone 13 years or older pays a regular adult fare. The following program determines how much a passenger should pay:

```python
# airfare.py
age = int(input('How old are you? '))
if age <= 2:
    print(' free')
elif 2 < age < 13:
    print(' child fare)
else:
    print('adult fare')
```

After Python gets age from the user, it enters the if/elif-statement and checks each condition one after the other in the order they are given. So first it checks if age is less than 2, and if so, it indicates that the flying is free and jumps out of the elif-condition. If age is not less than 2, then it checks the next elif-condition to see if age is between 2 and 13. If so, it prints the appropriate message and jumps out of the if/elif-statement. If neither the if-condition nor the elif-condition is True, then it executes the code in the else-block.

✔ Tips

- elif is short for *else if*, and you can use as many elif-blocks as needed.

- As usual, each of the code blocks in an if/elif-statement must be consistently indented the same amount. Not only does Python require this indentation so that it can recognize the code blocks, but the consistent indentation makes it easy for people to recognize the if/elif-conditions and their corresponding code blocks.

- As with a regular if-statement, the else-block is optional. In an if/elif-statement *with* an else-block, *exactly one* of the if/elif-blocks will be executed. If there is no else-block, then it is possible that none of the conditions are True, in which case none of the if/elif-blocks are executed.

- An if/elif-statement must have exactly one if-block, zero or more elif-blocks, and zero or one else-blocks.

Conditional expressions

Python has one more logical operator that some programmers like (and some don't!). It's essentially a shorthand notation for if-statements that can be used directly within expressions. Consider this code:

```
food = input("What's your favorite
→ food? ")
reply = 'yuck' if food == 'lamb' else
→ 'yum'
```

The expression on the right-hand side of = in the second line is called a *conditional expression*, and it evaluates to either 'yuck' or 'yum'. It's equivalent to the following:

```
food = input("What's your favorite
→ food? ")
if food == 'lamb':
    reply = 'yuck'
else:
    reply = 'yum'
```

Conditional expressions are usually shorter than the corresponding if/else-statements, although not quite as flexible or easy to read. In general, you should use them when they make your code simpler.

Loops

Now we turn to loops, which are used to repeatedly execute blocks of code. Python has two main kinds of loops: *for-loops* and *while-loops*. For-loops are generally easier to use and less error prone than while-loops, although not quite as flexible.

For-loops

The basic for-loop repeats a given block of code some specified number of times. For example, this snippet of code prints the numbers 0 to 9 on the screen:

```
# count10.py
for i in range(10):
    print(i)
```

The first line of a for-loop is called the *for-loop header*. A for-loop always begins with the keyword for. After that comes the *loop variable*, in this case i. Next is the keyword in, typically (but not always) followed by range(n) and a terminating : token. A for-loop repeats its *body*, the code block underneath it, exactly n times.

Each time the loop executes, the loop variable i is set to be the next value. By default, the initial value of i is 0, and it goes up to n - 1 (not n!) by ones. Starting numbering at 0 is fairly common in programming, although it is surprising at first.

If you want to change the starting value of the loop, add a starting value to range:

```
for i in range(5, 10):
    print(i)
```

This prints the numbers from 5 to 9.

Thinking about for-loops as printing a list of numbers is a good way to learn what they do. We will see many more examples of for-loops throughout this book.

Lingo Alert

Programmers often use the variable i because it is short for *index*, and is also commonly used in mathematics. When we start using loops within loops, it is common to use j and k as other loop variable names.

Of course, you can, and should, use any loop variable name that makes your code more readable.

✔ Tips

■ If you want to print the numbers from 1 to 10 (instead of 0 to 9), there are two common ways of doing so. One is to change the start and end of the range:

```
for i in range(1, 11):
    print(i)
```

Or, you can add 1 to i inside the loop body:

```
for i in range(10):
    print(i + 1)
```

■ If you would like to print numbers in *reverse* order, there are again two standard ways of doing so. The first is to set the range parameters like this:

```
for i in range(10, 0, -1):
    print(i)
```

Notice that the first value of range is 10, the second value is 0, and the third value, called the *step*, is -1. Alternatively, you can use a simpler range and modify i in the loop body:

```
for i in range(10):
    print(10 - i)
```

■ For-loops are actually more general than described in this section: They can be used with any kind of *iterator*, which is a special kind of programming object that returns values. For instance, we will see later that for-loops are the easiest way to read the lines of a text file.

While-loops

The second kind of Python loop is a *while-loop*. Consider this program:

```python
# while10.py
i = 0
while i < 10:
    print(i)
    i = i + 1  # add 1 to i
```

This prints out the numbers from 0 to 9 on the screen. It is noticeably more complicated than a for-loop, but it is also more flexible.

The while-loop itself begins on the line beginning with the keyword `while`; this line is called the *while-loop header*, and the indented code underneath it is called the *while-loop body*. The header always starts with `while` and is followed by the *while-loop condition*. This condition is a Boolean expression that returns `True` or `False`.

The flow of control through a while-loop goes like this: First, Python checks if the loop condition is `True` or `False`. If it's `True`, it executes the body; if it's `False`, it skips over the body (that is, it jumps out of the loop) and runs whatever statements appear afterward. When the condition is `True`, the body is executed, and then Python checks the condition again. As long as the loop condition is `True`, Python keeps executing the loop. **Figure 4.2** shows a flow chart for this program.

The very first line of the sample program is i = 0, and in the context of a loop it is known as an *initialization statement*, or an *initializer*. Unlike with for-loops, which automatically initialize their loop variable, it is the programmer's responsibility to give initial values to any variables used by a while-loop.

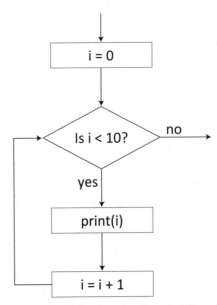

Figure 4.2 This is a flow chart for code that counts from 0 to 9. Notice that when the loop condition is `False` (that is, the *no* branch is taken in the decision box), the arrow does not go into a box. That's because in our sample code there is nothing after the while-loop.

The last line of the loop body is i = i + 1. As it says in the source code comment, this line causes i to be incremented by 1. Thus, i increases as the loop executes, which guarantees that the loop will eventually stop. In the context of a while-loop, this line is called an *increment,* or *incrementer,* since its job is to increment the loop variable.

The general form of a while-loop is shown in the flow chart of **Figure 4.3**.

Even though almost all while-loops need an initializer and an incrementer, Python does not require that you include them. It is entirely up to you, the programmer, to remember these lines. Even experienced programmers find that while-loop initializers and incrementers are a common source of errors.

```
initializer_block
while cond:
    body_block
after_block
```

Figure 4.3 A flow chart for the general form of a while-loop. Note that the incrementer is not shown explicitly: It is embedded somewhere in body_block often (but not always) at the end of that block.

✔ Tips

- While-loops are *extremely* flexible. You can put any code whatsoever before a while-loop to do whatever kind of initialization is necessary. The loop condition can be *any* Boolean expression, and the incrementer can be put *anywhere* within the while-loop body, and it can do whatever you like.

- A loop that never ends is called an *infinite loop*. For instance, this runs forever:

```
while True:
    print('spam')
```

- Some programmers like to use infinite loops as a quick way to write a loop. However, in practice, such loops often become complex and hard to understand. Plus, they are usually a sign of an incorrect (or missing!) initializer or incrementer.

- While-loops are powerful but error prone. Thus many Python programmers try to use for-loops whenever possible and use while-loops only when absolutely necessary.

- While-loops can be written with an else-block. However, this unusual feature is rarely used in practice, so we haven't discussed it. If you are curious, you can read about it in the online Python documentation—for example, http://docs.python.org/dev/3.0/reference/compound_stmts.html.

Comparing For-Loops and While-Loops

Let's take a look at a few examples of how for-loops and while-loops can be used to solve the same problems. Plus we'll see a simple program that can't be written using a for-loop.

Calculating factorials

Factorials are numbers of the form $1 \times 2 \times 3 \times \ldots \times n$, and they tell you how many ways n objects can be arranged in a line. For example, the letters ABCD can be arranged in $1 \times 2 \times 3 \times 4 = 24$ different ways. Here's one way to calculate factorials using a for-loop:

```
# forfact.py
n = int(input('Enter an integer >= 0: '))
fact = 1
for i in range(2, n + 1):
    fact = fact * i
print(str(n) + ' factorial is ' +
→ str(fact))
```

Here's another way to do it using a while-loop:

```
# whilefact.py
n = int(input('Enter an integer >= 0: '))
fact = 1
i = 2
while i <= n:
    fact = fact * i
    i = i + 1
print(str(n) + ' factorial is ' +
→ str(fact))
```

Both of these programs behave the same from the user's perspective, but the internals are quite different. As is usually the case, the while-loop version is a little more complicated than the for-loop version.

✔ Tips

- In mathematics, the notation *n!* is used to indicate factorials. For example, 4! = $1 \times 2 \times 3 \times 4 = 24$. By definition, 0! = 1. Interestingly, there is *no* simple shortcut formula for calculating large factorials.

- Python has no maximum integer, so you can use these programs to calculate very large factorials. For example, a deck of cards can be arranged in exactly 52! ways:

```
Enter an integer >= 0: 52
52 factorial is 80658175170943878571
→ 66063685640376697528950544088832778
→ 24000000000000
```

Summing numbers from the user

The following programs ask the user to enter some numbers, and then return their sum. Here is a version using a for-loop:

```
# forsum.py
n = int(input('How many numbers to
→ sum? '))
total = 0
for i in range(n):
    s = input('Enter number ' + str(i +
    → 1) + ': ')
    total = total + int(s)
print('The sum is ' + str(total))
```

Here's a program that does that same thing using a while-loop:

```
# whilesum.py
n = int(input('How many numbers to
→ sum? '))
total = 0
i = 1
while i <= n:
    s = input('Enter number ' + str(i)
    → + ': ')
    total = total + int(s)
    i = i + 1
print('The sum is ' + str(total))
```

Again, the while-loop version is a little more complex than the for-loop version.

✔ Tip

- These programs assume that the user is entering integers. Floating point numbers will be truncated when int(s) is called. Of course, you can easily change this to float(s) if you want to allow floating point numbers.

Summing an unknown number of numbers

Now here's something that can't be done with the for-loops we've introduced so far. Suppose we want to let users enter a list of numbers to be summed without asking them ahead of time how many numbers they have. Instead, they just type the string `'done'` when they have no more numbers to add. Here's how to do it using a while-loop:

```python
# donesum.py
total = 0
s = input('Enter a number (or "done"): ')
while s != 'done':
    num = int(s)
    total = total + num
    s = input('Enter a number (or
    → "done"): ')
print('The sum is ' + str(total))
```

The idea here is to keep asking users to enter a number, quitting only when they enter `'done'`. The program doesn't know ahead of time how many times the loop body will be executed.

Notice a few more details:

◆ We must call `input` in two different places: before the loop and inside the loop body. This is necessary because the loop condition decides whether or not the input is a number or `'done'`.

◆ The ordering of the statements in the loop body is very important. If the loop condition is `True`, then we know `s` is not `'done'`, and so we assume it is an integer. Thus we can convert it to an integer, add it to the running total, and then ask the user for more input.

◆ We convert the input string `s` to an integer only *after* we know `s` is not the string `'done'`. If we had written

```
s = int(input('Enter a number (or
→ "done"): '))
```

as we had previously, the program would crash when the user typed `'done'`.

◆ There is no need for the `i` counter variable anymore. In the previous summing programs, `i` was needed to track how many numbers had been entered so far. As a general rule of thumb, a program with fewer variables is easier to read, debug, and extend.

Breaking Out of Loops and Blocks

The break statement is a handy way for exiting a loop from anywhere within the loop's body. For example, here is an alternative way to sum an unknown number of numbers:

```python
# donesum_break.py
total = 0
while True:
    s = input('Enter a number (or
    → "done"): ')
    if s == 'done':
        break  # jump out of the loop
    num = int(s)
    total = total + num
print('The sum is ' + str(total))
```

The while-loop condition is simply True, which means it will loop forever unless break is executed. The only way for break to be executed is if s equals 'done'.

A major advantage of this program over donesum.py is that the input statement is not repeated. But a major disadvantage is that the reason for why the loop ends is buried in the loop body. It's not so hard to see it in this small example, but in larger programs break statements can be tricky to see. Furthermore, you can have as many breaks as you want, which adds to the complexity of understanding the loop.

Generally, it is wise to avoid the break statement, and to use it only when it makes your code simpler or clearer.

A relative of break is the continue statement: When continue is called inside a loop body, it immediately jumps up to the loop condition—thus continuing with the next iteration of the loop. It is a little less common than break, and generally it should be avoided altogether.

✔ Tips

- Both break and continue also work with for-loops.

- When you have a loop within a loop, both break and continue apply only to the innermost enclosing loop.

Loops Within Loops

Loops within loops, also known as *nested loops*, occur frequently in programming, so it is helpful to see a few examples. For instance, here's a program that prints out the times tables up to 10:

```
# timestable.py
for row in range(1, 10):
    for col in range(1, 10):
        prod = row * col
        if prod < 10:
            print(' ', end = '')
        print(row * col, ' ', end = '')
    print()
```

Look carefully at the indentation of the code in this program: It's how you tell what statements belong to what blocks. The final `print()` statement lines up with the second `for`, meaning it is part of the outer for-loop (but not the inner).

Note that the statement `if prod < 10` is used to make the output look neatly formatted. Without it, the numbers won't line up nicely.

✔ Tips

- When using nested loops, be careful with loop index variables: Do not accidentally reuse the same variable for a different loop. Most of the time, every individual loop needs its own control variables.

- You can nest as many loops within loops as you need, although the complexity increases greatly as you do so.

- As mentioned previously, if you use `break` or `continue` with nested loops, `break` only breaks out of the innermost loop, and `continue` only "continues" the innermost loop.

FUNCTIONS

A *function* is a reusable chunk of code. It is a block of code with a name that takes input, provides output, and can be stored in files for later use. Pretty much any useful piece of Python code is stored in a function.

Python has excellent support for functions. For instance, it provides many ways to pass data into a function. It also lets you include documentation strings within the function itself so that you—or other programmers—can always read how the function works.

Once we learn about functions, we will be using them constantly. Thus it is important that you have a good grasp of how they work. As we will soon see, we must master a handful of details in order to completely understand functions. With practice, these details soon become second nature, so be sure to try out the examples from this chapter.

Calling Functions

We've been calling functions quite a bit so far, so let's take a moment to look a little more carefully at a *function call*.

Consider the built-in function pow(x, y), which calculates x ** y—that is to say, x raised to the power y:

```
>>> pow(2, 5)
32
```

Here, we say that pow is the *function name*, and that the values 2 and 5 are *arguments* that are *passed into* pow. The value 32 is the *return value*, so we say that pow(2, 5) *returns* 32. **Figure 5.1** gives a high-level overview of a function call.

When you call a function within an expression, Python essentially replaces the function call with its return value. For example, the expression pow(2, 5) + 8 is the same as 32 + 8, which evaluates to 40.

When a function takes no input (that is to say, it has zero arguments), you must still include the round brackets ( ) after the function name:

```
>>> dir()
['__builtins__', '__doc__',
→ '__name__', '__package__']
```

The ( ) tells Python to execute the function. If you leave off the ( ), then you get this:

```
>>> dir
<built-in function dir>
```

Without the ( ), Python does not execute the dir function and instead tells you that dir labels a function. The underlying idea of function names and variable names is the same: A function name labels a special *function object*, while a variable name labels data (such as strings or numbers).

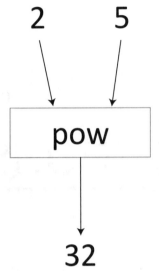

Figure 5.1 It's often useful to think of functions as being black boxes that accept an input (2 and 5 in this case) and return an output (32). From the point of view of a programmer calling the pow function, there is no (easy) way to see inside of pow. All we know is what the documentation tells us, and what the function does when we call it.

Calculating Powers

Calling pow(x, y) is the same as calling x ** y. You may notice that pow(0, 0) (and also 0 ** 0) is 1 in Python, and this has been a matter of some debate. According to some mathematicians, pow(0, 0) ought to be *indeterminate*, or undefined. But others say that it is more sensible to define pow(0, 0) as 1. Python has obviously sided with the latter group.

One other detail about pow is that it allows you to call it with three values—for example, pow(x, y, z). This is equivalent to (x ** y) % z.

Functions that don't return a value

Some functions, such as print, are not meant to return values. Consider:

```
>>> print('hello')
hello
>>> x = print('hello')
hello
>>> x
>>> print(x)
None
```

Here the variable x has been assigned a special value called None. None indicates "no return value": It is not a string or a number, so you can't do any useful calculations with it.

Reassigning function names

You need to take care not to accidentally make a built-in function name refer to some other function or value. Unfortunately, Python never stops you from writing code like this:

```
>>> dir = 3
>>> dir
3
>>> dir()
Traceback (most recent call last):
  File "<pyshell#28>", line 1, in
  → <module>
    dir()
TypeError: 'int' object is not callable
```

Here we've made dir label the number 3, so the function object that dir used to refer to is no longer accessible! It has disappeared, and will only return once you restart Python.

On the plus side, the ability to reassign function names this way allows you to play advanced tricks like rewriting built-in functions. But we won't be doing any of that in this book—we'll always leave the built-in functions as they are.

Defining Functions

Now we turn to creating our own functions. As an example, let's write a function to calculate the area of a circle. Recall that a circle's area is pi times its radius squared. Here is a Python function that does this calculation:

```
# area.py
def area(radius):
    """ Returns the area of a circle with
    → the given radius.
    For example:

    >>> area(5.5)
    95.033177771091246
    """

    import math
    return math.pi * radius ** 2
```

Save this function inside a Python file (area.py would be a good name); then load it into the IDLE editor and run it by pressing F5. If everything is typed correctly, a prompt should appear and nothing else; a function is not executed until you call it. To call it, just type the name of the function, with the radius in brackets:

```
>>> area(1)
3.1415926535897931
>>> area(5.5)
95.033177771091246
>>> 2 * (area(3) + area(4))
157.07963267948966
```

The area function can be called just like any other function, the difference being that *you* have written the function and so *you* have control over what it does and how it works.

Naming Functions

As with variable names, a function name must be one or more characters long and consist of letters, numbers, or the underscore (_) character. The first character of the name *cannot* be a number.

In general, give functions simple English names that hint at their *purpose*. Don't make them too long or too short. Other programmers reading your code or using your functions (including you, a few months down the road!) will thank you for choosing helpful names.

Parts of a function

Let's look at each part of the `area` function. The first line, the one that begins with `def`, is called the *function header*; all the code indented beneath the header is called the *function body*.

Function headers always begin with the keyword `def` (short for *definition*), followed by a space, and then the *name* of the function (in this case, `area`). Function names follow essentially the same rules as names for variables.

After the function name comes the function *parameter list*: This is a list of variable names that label the input to the function. The `area` function has a single input, `radius`, although a function can have any number of inputs. If a function has 0 inputs, then only the round brackets are written, `( )`.

Finally, like loops and if-statements, a function header ends with a colon (`:`).

After the function header comes an optional *documentation string*, or *doc string* for short. A doc string contains documentation for the programmer. It briefly explains what the function will do, and it may include examples or other helpful information. While doc strings are optional, they are almost always a good idea: When you start writing a lot of functions, it is easy to forget exactly what they do and how they work, and a well-written doc string can be a good reminder.

After the doc string comes the main *body* of the function. This is simply an indented block of code that does whatever you need it to do. The code in this block is allowed to use the variables from the function header. Just as with if-statements and loops, the beginning and end of the body block are marked using consistent indentation.

A Formatting Convention

Python doc strings tend to follow a standard formatting convention. Triple quotes are used to mark the beginning and end of the doc string. The first line is a succinct one-line description of the function useful to a programmer. After the first line come more details and examples.

Extra Benefits of Doc Strings

Just as with built-in functions, you can easily access the doc strings for your own functions, like this:

```
>>> print(area.__doc__)
Returns the area of a circle with the
 given radius.
For example:
    >>> area(5.5)
    95.033177771091246
```

As you will see when you call `area` in the IDLE editor, IDLE automatically reads the function doc string and pops it up as an automatic tool tip.

Python also has a useful tool called *doctest* that can be used to automatically run example Python code found in doc strings. This is a good way to test your code, and to help ensure that the documentation accurately describes the function. We won't go into the details of doctest in this book, but it is easy to use and quite helpful, and you can read more about it here: http://docs.python.org/dev/3.0/library/doctest.html.

DEFINING FUNCTIONS

67

Finally, the function should *return* a value using the `return` keyword. When a `return` statement is executed, Python *jumps out of the function* and back to the point in the program where it was called.

In the case of the `area` function, the `return` statement is the last line of the function, and it simply returns the value of the area of a circle using the standard formula. Note that it uses the `radius` parameter in its calculation; the value for `radius` is set when the `area` function is called either elsewhere in the program or at the interactive command line.

A `return` is usually the last line of a function to be executed (the only time it isn't is when the function ends unexpectedly due to an *exception* being thrown, which we will talk about in a later chapter). You can put a `return` anywhere inside a function body, although it is typically the last physical line of the function.

A function is not required to have an explicit `return` statement. For example:

```
# hello.py
def say_hello_to(name):
    """ Prints a hello message.
    """
    cap_name = name.capitalize()
    print('Hello ' + cap_name + ', how
    → are you?')
```

If you don't put a `return` anywhere in a function, Python treats the function as if it ended with this line:

```
return None
```

The special value `None` is used to indicate that the function is not meant to be returning a useful value. This is fairly common: Functions are often used to perform tasks where the return values don't matter, such as printing output to the screen.

Lingo Alert

When a function makes a change in any way other than returning a value, we call that change a *side effect*. Printing to the screen, writing to a file, and playing a song are all examples of side effects.

A style of programming known as *functional programming* is characterized by its near-complete banishment of side effects. In functional programming, the only changes you can make are via return values. Python has a lot of support for functional programming, including the ability to define functions within functions and to pass functions as values to other functions. When used correctly, functional programming can be a very elegant and powerful way of writing programs.

While we won't be covering functional programming in detail in this book, it is nonetheless wise to avoid function side effects whenever possible.

Variable Scope

An important detail that functions bring up is the issue of *scope*. The scope of a variable or function is where in a program it is accessible, or visible. Consider these two functions:

```python
# local.py
def dist(x, y, a, b):
    import math
    s = (x - a) ** 2 + (y - b) ** 2
    return math.sqrt(s)

def rect_area(x, y, a, b):
    width = abs(x - a)
    height = abs(y - b)
    return width * height
```

Any variable assigned for the first time within a function is called a *local variable*. The function dist has one local variable, s, while rect_area has two local variables, width and height.

The parameters of a function are also considered local. Thus dist has a total of five local variables—x, y, a, b, and s; rect_area has a total of six. Notice that variables x, y, a, and b appear in both functions, but they generally label different values.

Importantly, local variables are usable only within the function they are local to. No code outside of the function can access its local variables.

When a function ends, its local variables are automatically deleted.

Global variables

Variables declared outside of any function are called *global variables*, and they are readable anywhere by any function or code within the program. However, there is a wrinkle in reassigning global variables within functions you need to be aware of. Consider the following:

```
# global_error.py
name = 'Jack'

def say_hello():
    print('Hello ' + name + '!')

def change_name(new_name):
    name = new_name
```

The variable name is a global variable because it is not declared inside any function. The say_hello() function reads the value of name and prints it to the screen as you would expect:

```
>>> say_hello()
Hello Jack!
```

However, things don't work as expected when you call change_name:

```
>>> change_name('Piper')
>>> say_hello()
Hello Jack!
```

Nothing changed—name still labels the value 'Jack'. The problem is that Python treated name inside the change_name function as being a local variable, and so ignored the global name variable.

To access the global variable, you must use the global statement:

```
# global_correct.py
name = 'Jack'

def say_hello():
    print('Hello ' + name + '!')

def change_name(new_name):
    global name
    name = new_name
```

This makes all the difference. Both functions now work as expected:

```
>>> say_hello()
Hello Jack!
>>> change_name('Piper')
>>> say_hello()
Hello Piper!
```

Using a main Function

It is usually a good idea to use at least one function in any Python program you write: main( ). A main( ) function is, by convention, assumed to be the starting point of your program. For instance, it's convenient to write the password program we saw in the previous chapter using a main function

```
# password2.py
def main():
    pwd = input('What is the password? ')
    if pwd == 'apple':
        print('Logging on ...')
    else:
        print('Incorrect password.')

    print('All done!')
```

Notice that all the code is indented underneath the main function header.

When you run password2.py in IDLE, nothing happens—only the prompt appears. You must type main( ) to execute the code within in it.

The advantage of using a main function is that it is now easier to rerun programs and pass in input values.

Main in Other Languages

The idea of using a main function is quite common, and some other programming languages, notably C, C++, and Java, actually define the use of main as part of the language. In Python, however, main is entirely optional, and used only as a helpful convention.

Figure 5.2 The state of memory after setting x to 3 and y to 4.

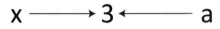

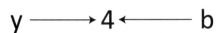

Figure 5.3 The state of memory just after add(x, y) is called, and a and b have been set to refer to the values of x and y, respectively.

Function Parameters

Parameters are used to pass input into a function, and Python has several kinds of parameters. First, though, we will look at the common way that all parameters are passed in Python.

Pass by reference

Python passes parameters to a function using a technique known as *pass by reference*. This means that when you pass parameters, the function refers to the *original* passed values using new names. For example, consider this simple program:

```
# reference.py
def add(a, b):
    return a + b
```

Run IDLE's interactive command line and type this:

```
>>> x, y = 3, 4
>>> add(x, y)
7
```

After you set x and y in the first line, Python's memory looks like **Figure 5.2**. Now when add(x, y) is called, Python creates two new variables, a and b, that refer to the values of x and y (**Figure 5.3**). The values are assigned in the order they occur—thus a refers to x because x is the first argument. Notice that the values are *not* copied: They are simply given new names that the function uses to refer to them.

After a and b are summed and the function returns, references a and b are automatically deleted. The original x and y are untouched throughout the entire function call.

Pass by Value

Another way to pass parameters is to use *pass by value*. When a parameter is passed by value, a *copy* of it is made and passed to the function. If the value being passed is large, the copying can take up a lot of time and memory. Python, however, does not support pass by value.

FUNCTION PARAMETERS

An important example

Passing by reference is simple and efficient, but there are some things it cannot do. For example, consider this plausibly named function:

```
# reference.py
def set1(x):
    x = 1
```

The intention is that it will set x to be the value 1. But when you try it, it does not work as expected:

```
>>> m = 5
>>> set1(m)
>>> m
5
```

Surprisingly, the value of m has *not* changed. The reason why is a consequence of pass by reference. It's helpful to break the example down into steps:

1. Assign 5 to m.

2. Call set1(m): Assign the value of x to the value of m (so now both m and x point to 5).

3. Assign 1 to m. Now the situation is as shown in **Figure 5.4**.

4. When the set1 function ends, x is deleted.

The variable m is simply not accessible within set1, so there is no way to change what it points to.

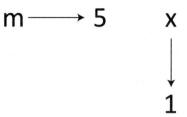

Figure 5.4 After x is assigned 1 in the function call set1(m), m is unchanged and still refers to its original value of 5. However, the local variable x has indeed been set to 1.

Default values

It's often useful to include a *default value* with a parameter.

To use default parameters:

◆ In your function header, assign a value to each parameter you want to have a default value. For example, here we have given the greeting parameter a default value of 'Hello':

```
# greetings.py
def greet(name, greeting = 'Hello'):
    print(greeting, name + '!')
```

◆ You can now call greet in two distinct ways, either with or without the greeting parameter value:

```
>>> greet('Bob')
Hello Bob!
>>> greet('Bob', 'Good morning')
Good morning Bob!
```

✔ Tips

■ Default parameters are quite handy and are used all the time in Python.

■ A function can use as many default parameters as it needs, although no parameter without a default value can appear before a parameter with one.

■ An important detail about default parameters is that they are evaluated only once, the first time they are called. In complicated programs, this can sometimes be the source of subtle bugs, so it is useful to keep this fact in mind.

FUNCTION PARAMETERS

Keyword parameters

Another useful way to specify parameters in Python is by using *keywords.*

To use keyword parameters:

◆ In the header of your function, give each parameter that you want to use as a keyword parameter a default value. For example:

```
# shopping.py
def shop(where = 'store',
         what = 'pasta',
         howmuch = '10 pounds'):
    print('I want you to go to the',
    → where)
    print('and buy', howmuch, 'of',
    → what + '.')
```

◆ To use keyword parameters when calling a function, call the function using the keyword form *param = value.* For example:

```
>>> shop()
I want you to go to the store
and buy 10 pounds of pasta.
>>> shop(what = 'towels')
I want you to go to the store
and buy 10 pounds of towels.
>>> shop(howmuch = 'a ton', what =
→ 'towels')
I want you to go to the store
and buy a ton of towels.
>>> shop(howmuch = 'a ton', what =
→ 'towels', where = 'bakery')
I want you to go to the bakery
and buy a ton of towels.
```

Keyword parameters have two big benefits. First, they make the parameter values clear, and thus help to make your programs easier to read. Second, the order in which you call keyword parameters does not matter. Both of these are quite helpful in functions with many parameters; for such functions it can be difficult to remember the exact order in which to put the parameters, and what they mean.

Modules

A *module* is collection of related functions and assignments.

To create a Python module:

◆ Create a .py file containing your functions and assignments. For example, here is a simple module for printing shapes to the screen:

```python
# shapes.py
"""A collection of functions
    for printing basic shapes.
"""

CHAR = '*'

def rectangle(height, width):
    """ Prints a rectangle.
    """

    for row in range(height):
        for col in range(width):
            print(CHAR, end = '')
        print()

def square(side):
    """ Prints a square.
    """

    rectangle(side, side)

def triangle(height):
    """ Prints a right triangle.
    """

    for row in range(height):
        for col in range(1, row + 2):
            print(CHAR, end = '')
        print()
```

The only difference between this and a regular Python program is the intended use: A module is a toolbox of helpful functions that you can use when writing other programs. Thus a module usually does not have a main( ) function.

- To use a module, you simply import it.
  For example:

```
>>> import shapes
>>> dir(shapes)
['CHAR', '__builtins__',
→ '__doc__', '__file__',
→ '__name__', '__package__',
→ 'rectangle', 'square', 'triangle']
>>> print(shapes.__doc__)
A collection of functions
for printing basic shapes.
>>> shapes.CHAR
'*'
>>> shapes.square(5)
*****
*****
*****
*****
*****
>>> shapes.triangle(3)
*
**
***
```

- You can also import everything at once:

```
>>> from shapes import *
>>> rectangle(3, 8)
********
********
********
```

Namespaces

A very useful fact about modules is that they form *namespaces*. A namespace is essentially a set of unique variable and function names. The names within a module are visible outside the module only when you use an `import` statement.

To see why this is important, suppose Jack and Sophie are working together on a large programming project. Jack is on the West Coast, and Sophie is on the East. They agree that Jack will put all his code in the module `jack.py`, and Sophie will put all her code into `sophie.py`. They work independently, and it turns out that they both wrote a function called `save_file(fname)`. However, only the headers of their functions are the same; they do radically different things. Having two functions with the same name is fine because the functions are in different modules, so the names are in different namespaces. The full name of Jack's function is `jack.save_file(fname)`, and the official name of Sophie's is `sophie.save_file(fname)`.

Thus modules support independent development, by preventing *name clashes*. Even if you are not working with other programmers, name clashes can be an annoying problem in your own programs, especially as they get larger and more complex.

Of course, you can still run into name clashes as follows:

```
>>> from jack import *
>>> from sophie import *
```

These kinds of import statements essentially dump everything from each module into the current namespace, overwriting anything with the same name as they go. Thus, it is generally wise to avoid `from . . . import *` statements in larger programs.

The Zen of Python

To see an interesting Python Easter egg, try importing the module `this` at the interactive command line:

```
>>> import this
```

STRINGS

6

After numbers, strings are the most important data type in Python. Strings are ubiquitous: You print them to the screen, you read them from the user, and, as we will see in Chapter 8, files are often treated as big strings. The World Wide Web can be thought of as a collection of Web pages, most of which consist of text. Plus the XML markup language, which is entirely text based, has become a popular file format for packages such as Microsoft Office.

Strings are a good example of an *aggregate data structure*, and they provide our first look at indexing and slicing—techniques that are used to extract substrings from strings.

The chapter also contains a brief introduction to Python's regular expression library, which is a supercharged mini-language designed for processing strings.

String Indexing

We've already introduced strings in Chapter 2, so you may want to go back to it if you need a refresher on string basics.

When working with strings, we often want to access their individual characters. For example, suppose you know that s is a string, and you want to access its constituent characters individually. *String indexing* is how you do it:

```
>>> s = 'apple'
>>> s[0]
'a'
>>> s[1]
'p'
>>> s[2]
'p'
>>> s[3]
'l'
>>> s[4]
'e'
```

Python uses *square brackets* to index strings: The number inside indicates which character to get (**Figure 6.1**). Python's index values always start at 0 and always end at one less than the length of the string.

So if s labels a string of length n, s[0] is the first character, s[1] is the second character, s[2] is the third character, and so on up to s[n-1], which is the last character.

If you try to index past the right end of the string, you will get an "out of range" error:

```
>>> s[5]
Traceback (most recent call last):
  File "<pyshell#6>", line 1, in <module>
    s[5]
IndexError: string index out of range
```

Figure 6.1 This diagram shows the index values for the string 'apple'. Square-bracket indexing notation is used to access individual characters within the string.

Why Start at 0?

Beginning programmers often find it odd that Python indexes begin at 0 instead of 1. It does take some getting used to and can be the source of *off-by-one errors* that plague many programmers. It can be helpful to think of an index value as *measuring the distance* from the first character of the string, just like a ruler (which also starts at 0). This makes some calculations with indexes a little simpler, and it also fits nicely with the % (mod) function, which is often used with index calculations and naturally returns 0s.

STRING INDEXING

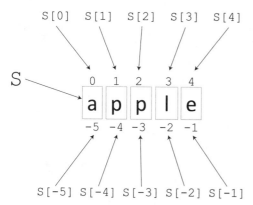

Figure 6.2 Python strings have both positive and negative indexes. In practice, programmers usually use whatever index is most convenient.

Negative indexing

Suppose instead of the first character of s, you want to access the last character of s. The ungainly expression s[len(s) - 1] works, but it seems rather complicated for accessing the last character of a string.

Fortunately, Python has a more convenient way of accessing characters near the right end of a string: *negative indexing*. The idea is that the characters of a string are indexed with negative numbers going from right to left:

```
>>> s = 'apple'
>>> s[-1]
'e'
>>> s[-2]
'l'
>>> s[-3]
'p'
>>> s[-4]
'p'
>>> s[-5]
'a'
```

Thus the last character of a string is simply s[-1]. **Figure 6.2** shows how negative index values work.

STRING INDEXING

Accessing characters with a for-loop

If you need to access every character of a string in sequence, a for-loop can be helpful. For example, this program calculates the sum of the character codes for a given string:

```
# codesum.py
def codesum1(s):
    """ Returns the sums of the character
        codes of s.
    """
    total = 0
    for c in s:
        total = total + ord(c)
    return total
```

Here is a sample call:

```
>>> codesum1('Hi there!')
778
```

When you use a for-loop like this, at the beginning of each iteration the loop variable c is set to be the next character in s. The indexing into s is handled automatically by the for-loop.

Compare codesum1 with this alternative implementation, which uses regular string indexing:

```
def codesum2(s):
    """ Returns the sums of the character
        codes of s.
    """
    total = 0
    for i in range(len(s)):
        total = total + ord(s[i])
    return total
```

This gives the same results as codesum1, but the implementation here is a little more complex and harder to read.

Characters

Strings consist of characters, and characters themselves turn out to be a surprisingly complex issue. As mentioned in Chapter 2, all characters have a corresponding character code that you can find using the `ord` function:

```
>>> ord('a')
97
>>> ord('b')
98
>>> ord('c')
99
```

Given a character code number, you can retrieve its corresponding character using the `chr` function:

```
>>> chr(97)
'a'
>>> chr(98)
'b'
>>> chr(99)
'c'
```

Character codes are assigned using the *Unicode* coding scheme, which is a large and complex standard for encoding all the symbols and characters that occur in all the world's languages.

The Rise of Unicode

In the 1960s, '70s, and '80s, the most popular character encoding scheme was *ASCII* (American Standard Code for Information Interchange). ASCII is far simpler than Unicode, but its fatal flaw is that it can represent only 256 different characters—enough for English and French and a few other similar languages, but nowhere near enough to represent the huge variety of characters and symbols found in other languages. For instance, Chinese alone has *thousands* of ideograms that could appear in text documents.

Essentially, Unicode provides a far larger set of character codes. Conveniently, Unicode mimics the ASCII code for the first 256 characters, so if you are only dealing with English characters (as we are in this book), you'll rarely need to worry about the details of Unicode. For more information, see the Unicode Home Page (www.unicode.org).

Escape characters

Not all characters have a standard visible symbol. For example, you can't see a new-line character, a return character, or a tab (although you can certainly see their *effects*). They are *whitespace characters*, characters that appear as blanks on the printed page.

To handle whitespace and other unprintable characters, Python uses a special notation called *escape sequences*, or *escape characters*. **Table 6.1** shows the most commonly used escape characters.

The backslash, single-quote, and double-quote escape characters are often needed for putting those characters into a string. For instance:

```
>>> print('\' and \" are quotes')
' and " are quotes
```

```
>>> print('\\ must be written \\\\')
\ must be written \\
```

The standard way in Python for ending a line is to use the \n character:

```
>>> print('one\ntwo\nthree')
one
two
three
```

It's important to realize that each escape character is only a single character. The leading \ is needed to tell Python that this is a special character, but that \ does not count as an extra character when determining a string's length. For example:

```
>>> len('\\')
1
>>> len('a\nb\nc')
5
```

Table 6.1

Some Common Escape Characters

CHARACTER	MEANING
\\	Backslash
\'	Single quote
\"	Double quote
\n	Newline (linefeed)
\r	Return (carriage return)
\t	Tab (horizontal tab)

Ending Lines

Different operating systems follow different standards for ending a line of text. For instance, Windows uses \r\n to mark the end of a line, while Mac OS X and Linux use just \n; Mac operating systems before Mac OS X used \r.

Most good editors handle at least the \r\n and \n styles. Occasionally you will run into programs (such as Notepad on Windows) that do not recognize one of these line-end formats, so text might appear all on the same line, contain extra line breaks, or have a ^M character at the end of each line. The easiest way to deal with this problem is to use a text editor that handles line endings correctly.

Slicing Strings

Slicing is how Python lets you extract a sub-string from a string. To slice a string, you indicate both the first character you want and one past the last character you want. For example:

```
>>> food = 'apple pie'
>>> food[0:5]
'apple'
>>> food[6:9]
'pie'
```

The indexing for slicing is the same as for accessing individual characters: The first index location is always 0, and the last is always one less than the length of the string. In general, s[begin:end] returns the sub-string starting at index begin and ending at index end - 1.

Note that if s is a string, then you can access the character at location i using either s[i] or s[i:i+1].

Slicing shortcuts

If you leave out the begin index of a slice,
then Python assumes you mean 0; and if
you leave off the end index, Python assumes
you want everything to the end of the string.
For instance:

```
>>> food = 'apple pie'
>>> food[:5]
'apple'
>>> food[6:]
'pie'
>>> food[:]
'apple pie'
```

Here's a useful example of slicing in practice.
This function returns the extension of a
filename.

```
# extension.py
def get_ext(fname):
    """ Returns the extension of file
        fname.
    """
    dot = fname.rfind('.')
    if dot == -1:  # no . in fname
        return ''
    else:
        return fname[dot + 1:]
```

Here's what get_ext does:

```
>>> get_ext('hello.text')
'text'
>>> get_ext('pizza.py')
'py'
>>> get_ext('pizza.old.py')
'py'
>>> get_ext('pizza')
''
```

The get_ext function works by determining the index position of the rightmost '.'
(hence the use of rfind to search for it from
right to left). If there is no '.' in fname, the
empty string is returned; otherwise, all the
characters from the '.' onward are returned.

SLICING STRINGS

Slicing with negative indexes

You can also use negative index values with slicing, although it's a bit confusing the first time you use it. For example:

```
>>> food = 'apple pie'
>>> food[-9:-4]
'apple'
>>> food[:-4]
'apple'
>>> food[-3:0]
''
>>> food[-3:]
'pie'
```

When working with negative slicing, or negative indexes in general, it is often useful to write the string you are working with on a piece of paper, and then write the positive and negative index values over the corresponding characters (as in Figure 6.2). While this does take an extra minute or two, it's a great way to prevent common indexing errors.

Standard String Functions

Python strings come prepackaged with a number of useful functions; use `dir` on any string (for example, `dir('')`) to see them all. While it's not necessary to memorize precisely what all these functions do, it is a good idea to have a general idea of their abilities so that you can use them when you need them. Thus, in this section we present a list of all the functions that come with a string, grouped together by type.

This is not meant to be a complete reference: A few infrequently used parameters are left out, and not every detail of every function is explained. For more complete details, read a function's doc string, or the online Python documentation (http://docs.python.org/dev/3.0/).

Testing functions

The first, and largest, group of functions is composed of ones that test if a string has a certain form. The testing functions in **Table 6.2** all return either `True` or `False`. Testing functions are sometimes called *Boolean functions*, or *predicates*.

Table 6.2

String-Testing Functions	
NAME	RETURNS TRUE JUST WHEN . . .
`s.endswith(t)`	s ends with string t
`s.startsswith(t)`	s starts with string t
`s.isalnum()`	s contains only letters or numbers
`s.isalpha()`	s contains only letters
`s.isdecimal()`	s contains only decimal characters
`s.isdigit()`	s contains only digits
`s.isidentifier()`	s is a valid Python identifier (that is, name)
`s.islower()`	s contains only lowercase letters
`s.isnumeric()`	s contains only numeric characters
`s.isprintable()`	s contains only printable characters
`s.isspace()`	s contains only whitespace characters
`s.istitle()`	s is a title-case string
`s.isupper()`	s contains only uppercase letters
`t in s`	s contains t as a substring

Table 6.3

String-Searching Functions	
NAME	RETURN VALUE
s.find(t)	-1, or index where t starts in s
s.rfind(t)	Same as find, but searches right to left
s.index(t)	Same as find, but raises ValueError if t is not in s
s.rindex(t)	Same as index, but searches right to left

Searching functions

As shown in **Table 6.3**, there are several ways to find substrings within a string. The difference between index and find functions is what happens when they don't find what they are looking for. For instance:

```
>>> s = 'cheese'
>>> s.index('eee')
Traceback (most recent call last):
  File "<pyshell#2>", line 1, in <module>
    s.index('eee')
ValueError: substring not found
>>> s.find('eee')
-1
```

The find function *raises* a ValueError; this is an example of *exception*, which we will talk about in more detail in Chapter 9. The index function returns -1 if the string being searched for is not found.

Normally, string-searching functions search the string from left to right, beginning to end. However, functions beginning with an r search from right to left. For example:

```
>>> s = 'cheese'
>>> s.find('e')
2
>>> s.rfind('e')
5
```

In general, find and index return the smallest index where the passed-in string starts, while rfind and rindex return the largest index where it starts.

Case-changing functions

Python gives you a variety of functions for changing the case of letters (**Table 6.4**). Keep in mind that Python *never* modifies a string: For all these functions, Python creates and returns a new string. We often talk as if the string were being modified, but this is only a convenient phrasing and does not mean the string is really being changed.

Formatting functions

The string-formatting functions listed in **Table 6.5** help you to make strings look nicer for presenting to the user or printing to a file.

The string `format` function is especially powerful, and it includes its own mini-language for formatting strings. To use `format`, you supply it variables or values—for example:

```
>>> '{0} likes {1}'.format('Jack', 'ice
→ cream')
'Jack likes ice cream'
```

The {0} and {1} in the string refer to the arguments in `format`: They are replaced by the values of the corresponding strings or variables. You can also refer to the names of keyword parameters:

```
>>> '{who} {pet} has fleas'.format(pet =
→ 'dog', who = 'my')
'my dog has fleas'
```

These examples show the most basic use of `format`; there are many other options for spacing strings, converting numbers to strings, and so on. All the details are provided in Python's online documentation (http://docs.python.org/dev/3.0/library/string.html#formatstrings).

Table 6.4

String-Searching Functions	
NAME	RETURNED STRING
s.capitalize()	s[0] is made uppercase
s.lower()	All letters of s are made lowercase
s.upper()	All letters of s are made uppercase
s.swapcase()	Lowercase letters are made uppercase, and uppercase letters are made lowercase
s.title()	Title-case version of s

Table 6.5

String-Formatting Functions	
NAME	RETURNED STRING
s.center(n, ch)	Centers s within a string of n ch characters
s.ljust(n, ch)	Left-justifies s within a string of n ch characters
s.rjust(n, ch)	Right-justifies s within a string of n ch characters
s.format(*vars*)	See text

Table 6.6

String-Stripping Functions

NAME	RETURNED STRING
s.strip(ch)	Removes all ch characters in t occurring at the beginning or end of s
s.lstrip(ch)	Removes all ch characters in t occurring at the beginning (that is, the left side) of s
s.rstrip(ch)	Removes all ch characters in t occurring at the end (that is, the right side) of s

Table 6.7

String-Splitting Functions

NAME	RETURNED STRING
s.partition(t)	Chops s into three strings (head, t, tail), where head is the substring before t and tail is the substring after t
s.rpartition(t)	Same as partition but searches for t starting at the right end of s
s.split(t)	Returns a list of substrings of s that are separated by t
s.rsplit(t)	Same as split, but starts searching for t at the right end of s
s.splitlines()	Returns a list of lines in s

Stripping functions

The stripping functions shown in **Table 6.6** are used for removing unwanted characters from the beginning or end of a string. By default, whitespace characters are stripped, and if a string argument is given, the characters in that string are stripped. For example:

```
>>> name = '  Gill    Bates    '
>>> name.lstrip()
'Gill    Bates    '
>>> name.rstrip()
'  Gill    Bates'
>>> name.strip()
'Gill    Bates'
>>> title = '_-_- Happy Days!! _-_-'
>>> title.strip()
'_-_- Happy Days!! _-_-'
>>> title.strip('_-')
' Happy Days!! '
>>> title.strip('_ -')
'Happy Days!!'
```

Splitting functions

The splitting functions listed in **Table 6.7** chop a string into substrings.

The partition and rpartition functions divide a string into three parts:

```
>>> url = 'www.google.com'
>>> url.partition('.')
('www', '.', 'google.com')
>>> url.rpartition('.')
('www.google', '.', 'com')
```

These partitioning functions always return a value consisting of three strings in the form (head, sep, tail). This kind of return value is an example of a *tuple*, which we will learn about in more detail in Chapter 7.

The `split` function divides a string into substrings based on a given separator string. For example:

```
>>> url = 'www.google.com'
>>> url.split('.')
['www', 'google', 'com']
>>> story = 'A long time ago, a princess
→ ate an apple.'
>>> story.split()
['A', 'long', 'time', 'ago,', 'a',
→ 'princess', 'ate', 'an', 'apple.']
```

The `split` function always returns a *list* of strings; a Python list always begins with a [and ends with a], and uses commas to separate elements. As we'll see in Chapter 7, lists and tuples are very similar, the main difference being that lists can be modified, but tuples are constant.

Replacement functions

Python strings come with two replacing functions, as shown in **Table 6.8**. Note that the `replace` function can easily be used to delete substrings within a string:

```
>>> s = 'up, up and away'
>>> s.replace('up', 'down')
'down, down and away'
>>> s.replace('up', '')
', and away'
```

Table 6.8

String-Replacement Functions	
NAME	**RETURNED STRING**
s.replace(old, new)	Replaces every occurrence of old within s with new
s.expandtabs(n)	Replaces each tab character in s with n spaces

Table 6.9

Other String Functions	
NAME	**RETURNED VALUE**
s.count(t)	Number of times t occurs within s
s.encode()	Sets the encoding of s; see the online documentation (http://docs.python.org/dev/3.0/library/stdtypes.html#str.encode) for more details
s.join(seq)	Concatenates the strings in seq, using s as a separator
s.maketrans(old, new)	Creates a translation table used to change the characters in old with the corresponding characters in new; note that s can be any string—it has no influence on the returned table
s.translate(table)	Makes the replacements in s using the given translation table (created with maketrans)
s.zfill(width)	Adds enough 0s to the left of s to make a string of length width

Other functions

Finally, **Table 6.9** lists the remaining string functions.

The `translate` and `maketrans` functions are useful when you need to convert one set of characters into another. For instance, here's one way to convert strings to "leet-speak":

```
>>> leet_table = ''.maketrans('EIOBT',
→ '31087')
>>> 'BE COOL. SPEAK LEET!'.translate
→ (leet_table)
'83 C00L. SP3AK L337!'
```

The online documentation (http://docs.python.org/dev/3.0/library/stdtypes.html) also explains how to replace more than single characters.

The `zfill` function is used for formatting numeric strings:

```
>>> '23'.zfill(4)
'0023'
>>> '-85'.zfill(5)
'-0085'
```

However, it's not a very flexible function, so most programmers prefer using one of Python's other string-formatting techniques.

The `join` function can be quite useful. It concatenates a sequence of strings, including a separator string. For example:

```
>>> ' '.join(['once', 'upon', 'a',
→ 'time'])
'once upon a time'
>>> '-'.join(['once', 'upon', 'a',
→ 'time'])
'once-upon-a-time'
>>> ''.join(['once', 'upon', 'a',
→ 'time'])
'onceuponatime'
```

STANDARD STRING FUNCTIONS

Regular Expressions

While Python strings provide many useful functions, real-world string processing often calls for more powerful tools.

Thus, programmers have developed a mini-language for advanced string processing known as *regular expressions*. Essentially, a regular expression is a way to *compactly* describe a *set* of strings. They can be used to efficiently perform common string-processing tasks such as matching, splitting, and replacing text. In this section, we'll introduce the basic ideas of regular expressions, as well as a few commonly used operators (**Table 6.10**).

Simple regular expressions

Consider the string `'cat'`. It represents a single string consisting of the letters *c*, *a*, and *t*. Now consider the regular expression `'cats?'`. Here, the ? does *not* mean an English question mark but instead represents a regular expression operator, meaning that the character to its immediate left is optional. Thus the regular expression `'cats?'` describes a set of two strings: `'cat'` and `'cats'`.

Another regular expression operator is |, which means "or." For example, the regular expression `'a|b|c'` describes the set of three strings `'a'`, `'b'`, and `'c'`.

The regular expression `'a*'` describes an infinite set of strings: `''`, `'a'`, `'aa'`, `'aaa'`, `'aaaa'`, `'aaaaa'`, and so on. In other words, `'a*'` describes the set of all strings consisting of a sequence of 0 or more `'a'`s. The regular expression `'a+'` is the same as `'a*'` but excludes the empty string `''`.

Finally, within a regular expression you can use round brackets to indicate what substring an operator ought to apply to. For example, the regular expression `'(ha)+!'` describes these strings: `'ha!'`, `'haha!'`, `'hahaha!'`, and so on. In contrast, `'ha+!'`

Table 6.10

OPERATOR	SET OF STRINGS DESCRIBED
Some Regular Expression Operators	
xy?	x, xy
x|y	x, y
x*	'', x, xx, xxx, xxxx, …
x+	x, xx, xxx, xxxx, …

describes a very different set: `'ha!'`, `'haa!'`, `'haaa!'`, and so on.

You can mix and match these (and many other) regular expression operators in any way you want. This turns out to be a very useful way to describe many commonly occurring types of strings, such as phone numbers and e-mail addresses.

Matching with regular expressions

A common application of regular expressions is string matching. For example, suppose you are writing a program where the user must enter a string such as `done` or `quit` to end the program. To help recognize these strings, you could write a function like this:

```
# allover.py
def is_done1(s):
    return s == 'done' or s == 'quit'
```

Using regular expressions, an identically behaving function might look like this:

```
# allover.py
import re  # use regular expressions

def is_done2(s):
    return re.match('done|quit', s)
  → != None
```

The first line of this new version imports Python's standard regular expression library. To match a regular expression, we use the `re.match(regex, s)` function, which returns `None` if `regex` does not match `s`, and a special regular expression *match object* otherwise. We don't care about the details of the match object in this example, so we only check to see if the result is `None` or not.

In such a simple example, the regular expression version is not much shorter or better than the first version; indeed, `is_done1` is probably preferable! However, regular expressions really

continues on next page

start to shine as your programs become larger and more complex. For instance, suppose we decide to add a few more possible stopping strings. For the regular expression version, we just rewrite the regular expression string to be, say, `'done|quit|over|finished|end|stop'`. In contrast, to make the same change to the first version, we'd need to include or `s ==` for each string we added, which would make for a very long line of code that would be hard to read.

Here's a more complex example. Suppose you want to recognize *funny strings*, which consist of one or more `'ha'` strings followed immediately by one or more `'!'`s. For example, `'haha!'`, `'ha!!!!!'`, and `'hahaha!!'` are all funny strings. It's easy to match these using regular expressions:

```
# funny.py
import re

def is_funny(s):
    return re.match('(ha)+!+', s) != None
```

Notice that the only essential difference between this is_funny and is_done2 is that a different regular expression is used inside `match`. If you try writing this same function without using regular expressions, you will quickly see how much work `'(ha)+!+'` is doing for us.

More regular expressions

We have barely scratched the surface of regular expressions: Python's re library is large and has many regular expression functions that can perform string-processing tasks such as matching, splitting, and replacing. There are also tricks for speeding up the processing of commonly used regular expressions, and numerous shortcuts for matching commonly used characters. The Python Regular Expression HOWTO, written by Andrew Kuchling, is a good place to get more details and examples (www.amk.ca/python/howto/regex/).

7

DATA STRUCTURES

In this chapter, we introduce the important idea of *data structures*: collections of values along with commonly performed functions. Python's programmer-friendly philosophy is to provide a few powerful and efficient data structures—*tuples*, *lists*, *dictionaries*, and *sets*—that can be combined as needed to make more complex ones.

In the previous chapter we discussed strings, which can be thought of as data structures restricted to storing sequences of characters. The data structures in this chapter can contain not just characters but almost any kind of data.

Python's two workhorse data structures are lists and dictionaries. Lists are simple, flexible data structures with many uses. Dictionaries, while necessarily a little more complex than lists, are an extremely efficient way to relate different pieces of data. Python provides a lot of support for both lists and dictionaries; in particular it has an extremely useful list-creation technique known as *list comprehensions*.

The type Command

It's occasionally useful to ask Python to check the data type of a value or a variable. This is easily done with the built-in type command:

```
>>> type(5)
<class 'int'>
>>> type(5.0)
<class 'float'>
>>> type('5')
<class 'str'>
>>> type(None)
<class 'NoneType'>
>>> type(print)
<class 'builtin_function_or_method'>
```

The term *class* comes from object-oriented programming. Roughly speaking, classes and types are synonymous. As we will see in Chapter 10, one of the great benefits of classes is that you can create your own.

One common application of the type command is to determine the type of data stored in a collection. Python lets you store values with different types in the same data structure. For example, you can store numbers and strings in the same list; in contrast, the popular Java programming language does not let you mix data types this way. A Java list must be all strings or all integers.

Sequences

In Python, a *sequence* is an ordered collection of values. Python comes with three built-in sequence types: *strings*, *tuples*, and *lists*.

One very nice feature of sequences is that they share the same indexing and slicing commands that we saw for strings in the previous chapter. Thus, all sequences have the following characteristics:

◆ They have positive indexes starting at 0 at their left end.

◆ They have negative indexes starting at -1 at their right end.

◆ They can have copies of sub-sequences made using slice notation. For example, `seq[begin:end]` returns a copy of the elements of `seq` starting at index location `begin` and ending at location `end` - `1`.

◆ They can be concatenated using + and *. The sequences must be of the same type for this to work—that is to say, you cannot concatenate a tuple and a list.

◆ They have their length determined by the `len` function. For example, `len(s)` is the number of items in sequence `s`.

◆ They test for membership using `x in s`—that is, `x in s` evaluates to `True` just when the element `x` is in the sequence `s`.

In practice, strings and lists are the most common kinds of sequences. Tuples have their uses but appear much less often.

It is often easy to write code that works with any sequence, no matter if it is a string, a list, or a tuple. For example, `seq[-1]` returns the last element of `seq` whether `seq` is a tuple, list, or string.

Order Matters

When we say that sequences are *ordered*, we mean that the order of the elements in the sequence matters. Strings are ordered because `'abc'` is different from `'acb'`. Later we will see that dictionaries and sets are not ordered: They only care if an item is inside of them, and in fact they can make no promises about their relative order.

How Big Can a Sequence Be?

Theoretically, there is no limit to the length of a sequence: It can contain as many items as needed. Practically, however, you are restricted by the amount of RAM available in your computer when Python is running.

SEQUENCES

Tuples

A *tuple* is an *immutable* sequence of 0 or more values. It can contain any Python value—even other tuples. Here are a few examples:

```
>>> items = (-6, 'cat', (1, 2))
>>> items
(-6, 'cat', (1, 2))
>>> len(items)
3
>>> items[-1]
(1, 2)
>>> items[-1][0]
1
```

As you can see, the items of a tuple are enclosed in round brackets and separated by commas. The empty tuple is represented by ( ), but tuples with a single item (*singleton tuples*) have the unusual notation (x,). For instance:

```
>>> type(())
<class 'tuple'>
>>> type((5,))
<class 'tuple'>
>>> type((5))
<class 'int'>
```

If you forget the comma at the end of a singleton tuple, you have not created a tuple: All you've done is put brackets around an expression, which means you are specifying its order of evaluation.

Trailing Commas

While singleton tuples *require* a trailing comma, a trailing comma is allowed, but not required, in longer tuples (and lists). For example, (1, 2, 3,) is the same as (1, 2, 3). Some programmers prefer to always include the trailing comma so that they never accidentally leave it out for singleton tuples.

Tuple immutability

As mentioned, tuples are immutable, meaning that once you've created a tuple, you cannot change it. This is not so unusual: Strings, integers, and floats are also immutable. If you do need to change a tuple, then you must create a new tuple that embodies the changes. For example, here's how you can chop off the first element of a tuple:

```
>>> lucky = (6, 7, 21, 77)
>>> lucky
(6, 7, 21, 77)
>>> lucky2 = lucky[1:]
>>> lucky2
(7, 21, 77)
>>> lucky
(6, 7, 21, 77)
```

On the plus side, immutability makes it impossible to accidentally modify a tuple, which helps prevent errors. On the minus side, making even the smallest change to a tuple requires copying essentially the whole thing, and this can waste valuable time and memory for large tuples. If you find yourself needing to make frequent modifications to a tuple, then you should be using a list instead.

TUPLES

Tuple functions

Table 7.1 lists the most commonly used tuple functions. Compared with strings and lists, tuples have a relatively small number of functions. Here are some examples of how they are used:

```
>>> pets = ('dog', 'cat', 'bird', 'dog')
>>> pets
('dog', 'cat', 'bird', 'dog')
>>> 'bird' in pets
True
>>> 'cow' in pets
False
>>> len(pets)
4
>>> pets.count('dog')
2
>>> pets.count('fish')
0
>>> pets.index('dog')
0
>>> pets.index('bird')
2
>>> pets.index('mouse')
Traceback (most recent call last):
  File "<pyshell#41>", line 1, in
  → <module>
    pets.index('mouse')
ValueError: tuple.index(x): x not in
→ list
```

As with strings, you can use + and * to concatenate tuples:

```
>>> tup1 = (1, 2, 3)
>>> tup2 = (4, 5, 6)
>>> tup1 + tup2
(1, 2, 3, 4, 5, 6)
>>> tup1 * 2
(1, 2, 3, 1, 2, 3)
```

Table 7.1

Tuple Functions	
NAME	**RETURN VALUE**
x in tup	True if x is an element of tup, False otherwise
len(tup)	Number of elements in tup
tup.count(x)	Number of times element x occurs in tup
tup.index(x)	Index location of the first (leftmost) occurrence of x in tup; if x is not in tup, raises a ValueError exception

Lists

Lists are essentially the same as tuples but with one key difference: Lists are *mutable*. That is, you can add, remove, or modify elements to a list without making a copy. In practice, lists are used far more frequently than tuples (indeed, some Python programmers are only faintly aware that tuples exist!).

The elements of a list are separated by commas and enclosed in square brackets. As with strings and tuples, you can easily get the length of a list (using len), and concatenate lists (using + and *):

```
>>> numbers = [7, -7, 2, 3, 2]
>>> numbers
[7, -7, 2, 3, 2]
>>> len(numbers)
5
>>> numbers + numbers
[7, -7, 2, 3, 2, 7, -7, 2, 3, 2]
>>> numbers * 2
[7, -7, 2, 3, 2, 7, -7, 2, 3, 2]
```

And just as with strings and tuples, you can use indexing and slicing to access individual elements and sublists:

```
>>> lst = [3, (1,), 'dog', 'cat']
>>> lst[0]
3
>>> lst[1]
(1,)
>>> lst[2]
'dog'
>>> lst[1:3]
[(1,), 'dog']
>>> lst[2:]
['dog', 'cat']
>>> lst[-3:]
[(1,), 'dog', 'cat']
>>> lst[:-3]
[3]
```

Notice that lists can contain any kinds of values: numbers, strings, or even other sequences. The *empty list* is denoted by [], and a singleton list containing just one element x is written [x] (in contrast to tuples, no trailing comma is necessary for a singleton list).

Mutability

As mentioned earlier, mutability is the key feature that distinguishes lists from tuples. For example:

```
>>> pets = ['frog', 'dog', 'cow',
→ 'hamster']
>>> pets
['frog', 'dog', 'cow', 'hamster']
>>> pets[2] = 'cat'
>>> pets
['frog', 'dog', 'cat', 'hamster']
```

As you can see, this sets the second element of the list pets to point to 'cat'. The string 'cow' gets replaced and is automatically deleted by Python.

Figure 7.1 shows a helpful diagrammatic representation of a list. Just as with variables, it is important to understand that the elements of a list only *point* to their values and do not actually contain them.

The fact that lists point to their values can be the source of some surprising behavior. Consider this nasty example:

```
>>> snake = [1, 2, 3]
>>> snake[1] = snake
>>> snake
[1, [...], 3]
```

Here, we've made an element of a list point to the list itself: We've created a *self-referential data structure*. The [...] in the printout indicates that Python recognizes the self-reference and does not stupidly print the list forever(!). **Figure 7.2** shows diagrammatically what snake looks like.

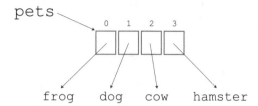

Figure 7.1 A Python list points to its values.

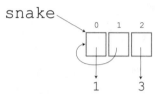

Figure 7.2 A self-referential list. Note that the second element is not pointing to the first element of the list, but to the entire list itself.

Lingo Alert

Many Python programmers speak as if a list *contains* its elements. While that is not technically accurate, it is a common and convenient phrasing. Much of the time it does not cause any confusion. But when it comes to finding errors in programs that process lists, it is often essential to understand that lists actually point to their values and don't contain them.

LISTS

Table 7.2

List Functions	
NAME	RETURN VALUE
s.append(x)	Appends x to the end of s
s.count(x)	Returns the number of times x appears in s
s.extend(lst)	Appends each item of lst to s
s.index(x)	Returns the index value of the leftmost occurrence of x
s.insert(i, x)	Inserts x before index location i (so that s[i] == x)
s.pop(i)	Removes and returns the item at index i in s
s.remove(x)	Removes the leftmost occurrence of x in s
s.reverse()	Reverses the order of the elements of s
s.sort()	Sorts the elements of s into increasing order

List Functions

Lists come with many useful functions (**Table 7.2**). All of these functions, except for count (which just returns a number), modify the list you call them with. Thus, these are *mutating functions*, so it pays to change your lists carefully. It is distressingly easy, for instance, to accidentally delete a wrong element or insert a new value at the wrong place.

The append function is a useful way to add elements to a list. One common programming pattern is to create an empty list at the beginning of a function and then add values to it in the rest of the function. For example, here is a function that creates a string of messages based on a list of input numbers:

```
# numnote.py
def numnote(lst):
    msg = []
    for num in lst:
        if num < 0:
            s = str(num) + ' is negative'
        elif 0 <= num <= 9:
            s = str(num) + ' is a digit'
        msg.append(s)
    return msg
```

For example:

```
>>> numnote([1, 5, -6, 22])
['1 is a digit', '5 is a digit',
'-6 is negative']
```

To print the messages on their own individual lines, you could do this:

```
>>> for msg in numnote([1, 5, -6, 22]):
→ print(msg)
1 is a digit
5 is a digit
-6 is negative
```

Or even this:

```
>>> print('\n'.join(numnote([1, 5, -6,
→ 22])))
1 is a digit
5 is a digit
-6 is negative
```

The extend function is similar to append, but it takes an entire sequence as input:

```
>>> lst = []
>>> lst.extend('cat')
>>> lst
['c', 'a', 't']
>>> lst.extend([1, 5, -3])
>>> lst
['c', 'a', 't', 1, 5, -3]
```

The pop function removes an element at a given index position and then returns it. For example:

```
>>> lst = ['a', 'b', 'c', 'd']
>>> lst.pop(2)
'c'
>>> lst
['a', 'b', 'd']
>>> lst.pop()
'd'
>>> lst
['a', 'b']
```

Lingo Alert

In computer programming, the term *pop* usually refers to the act of removing the last element of a list. The related term, *push*, refers to adding an element to the same end (that is, exactly what Python's append does). When push and pop are used on the same list, we often refer to it as a *stack*: We say that items are pushed onto the *top* of the stack and then popped from the top of the stack. Despite their simplicity, stacks form the basis of a number of more advanced programming behaviors, such as recursion and undo.

Notice that if you don't give pop an index, it removes and returns the element at the end of the list.

The remove(x) function removes the first occurrence of x from a list. However, it does not return x:

```
>>> lst = ['a', 'b', 'c', 'a']
>>> lst.remove('a')
>>> lst
['b', 'c', 'a']
```

As the name suggests, reverse reverses the order of the elements of a list:

```
>>> lst = ['a', 'b', 'c', 'a']
>>> lst
['a', 'b', 'c', 'a']
>>> lst.reverse()
>>> lst
['a', 'c', 'b', 'a']
```

It's important to realize that reverse does not make a copy of the list: It actually moves the list pointers, so we say the reversal is done *in place*.

LIST FUNCTIONS

Sorting Lists

Sorting data is one of the most common things that computers do. Sorted data is usually easier to work with than unsorted data, for both humans and computers. For instance, finding the smallest element of a sorted list requires no searching at all: It is simply the first element of the list. Humans often prefer to see data in sorted order— just imagine a phone book that was not printed alphabetically!

In Python, sorting is most easily done using the list `sort()` function, which is extremely efficient: In practice, it can be used to quickly sort lists with tens of thousands of elements. Like `reverse()`, `sort()` modifies the list in place:

```
>>> lst = [6, 0, 4, 3, 2, 6]
>>> lst
[6, 0, 4, 3, 2, 6]
>>> lst.sort()
>>> lst
[0, 2, 3, 4, 6, 6]
```

The sort function always sorts elements into ascending order, from smallest to largest. If you want the elements sorted in reverse order, from largest to smallest, the simple trick of calling reverse after sort works well:

```
>>> lst = ['up', 'down', 'cat', 'dog']
>>> lst
['up', 'down', 'cat', 'dog']
>>> lst.sort()
>>> lst
['cat', 'dog', 'down', 'up']
>>> lst.reverse()
>>> lst
['up', 'down', 'dog', 'cat']
```

Python also knows how to sort tuples and lists. For example:

```
>>> pts = [(1, 2), (1, -1), (3, 5),
→ (2, 1)]
>>> pts
[(1, 2), (1, -1), (3, 5), (2, 1)]
>>> pts.sort()
>>> pts
[(1, -1), (1, 2), (2, 1), (3, 5)]
```

Tuples (and lists) are sorted by their first element, then by their second element, and so on.

Lingo Alert

The order in which Python sorts a list of sequences is called *lexicographical ordering*. This is just a general term meaning "alphabetical order," except that it applies to any sequence of orderable values, not just letters. The idea is that elements are ordered by their initial element, then their second element, then their third element, and so on.

List Comprehensions

Lists are so used so frequently that Python provides a special notation for creating them called *list comprehensions*. For example, here's how to create a list of the squares of the numbers from 1 to 10 with a list comprehension:

```
>>> [n * n for n in range(1, 11)]
[1, 4, 9, 16, 25, 36, 49, 64, 81, 100]
```

The main advantage of this notation is that it is compact *and* readable. Compare this with equivalent code without a comprehension:

```
result = []
for n in range(1, 11):
    result.append(n * n)
```

Once you get the hang of them, list comprehensions are quick and easy to write, and you will find many uses for them.

More examples

Let's see a few more examples of comprehensions. If you want to double each number on the list and 7, you can do this:

```
>>> [2 * n + 7for n in range(1, 11)]
[9, 11, 13, 15, 17, 19, 21, 23, 25, 27]
```

Or if you want the first ten cubes:

```
>>> [n ** 3 for n in range(1, 11)]
[1, 8, 27, 64, 125, 216, 343, 512, 729,
→ 1000]
```

You can also use strings in comprehensions. For example:

```
>>> [c for c in 'pizza']
['p', 'i', 'z', 'z', 'a']
>>> [c.upper() for c in 'pizza']
['P', 'I', 'Z', 'Z', 'A']
```

A common application of comprehensions is to modify an existing list in some way. For instance:

```
>>> names = ['al', 'mei', 'jo', 'del']
>>> names
['al', 'mei', 'jo', 'del']
>>> cap_names = [n.capitalize() for n
→ in names]
>>> cap_names
['Al', 'Mei', 'Jo', 'Del']
>>> names
['al', 'mei', 'jo', 'del']
```

Filtered comprehensions

List comprehensions can be written with tests, which allow you to filter out elements from other lists. For example, the following comprehension returns a list containing just the positive elements of nums:

```
>>> nums = [-1, 0, 6, -4, -2, 3]
>>> result = [n for n in nums if n > 0]
>>> result
[6, 3]
```

Here's equivalent code without a comprehension:

```
result = []
nums = [-1, 0, 6, -4, -2, 3]
for n in nums:
    if n > 0:
        result.append(n)
```

Again, we see that list comprehensions are more compact and readable than a regular loop.

Here's a comprehension that removes all the vowels from a word written inside a function:

```
# eatvowels.py
def eat_vowels(s):
    """ Removes the vowels from s.
    """
    return ''.join([c for c in s
                    if c.lower() not in
                    → 'aeiou'])
```

It works like this:

```
>>> eat_vowels('Apple Sauce')
'ppl Sc'
```

The body of eat_vowels looks rather cryptic at first, and the trick to understanding it is to read it a piece at a time. First, look at the comprehension:

```
[c for c in s if c.lower() not in
'aeiou']
```

This is a filtered comprehension that scans through the characters of s one at a time. It converts each character to lowercase and then checks to see if it is a vowel. If it is a vowel, it is skipped and not added to the resulting list; otherwise, it is added.

The result of this comprehension is a list of strings, so we use join to concatenate all the strings into a single string that is then immediately returned.

Generator Expressions

There's one more simplification we could make to eat_vowels: The square brackets in the comprehension can be removed:

```
''.join(c for c in s
    if c.lower() not in 'aeiou')
```

The expression inside join is an example of a *generator expression*. In more advanced Python programming, generator expressions can be used to efficiently generate only the needed part of a list or sequence, with the elements being generated *on demand* instead of all at once as with a list comprehension.

LIST COMPREHENSIONS

Dictionaries

A Python *dictionary* is an extremely efficient data structure for storing *pairs* of values in the form *key:value*. For example:

```
>>> color = {'red' : 1, 'blue' : 2,
→ 'green' : 3}
>>> color
{'blue': 2, 'green': 3, 'red': 1}
```

The dictionary `color` has three members. One of them is `'blue':2`, where `'blue'` is the *key* and 2 is its associated *value*.

You access values in a dictionary by their keys:

```
>>> color['green']
3
>>> color['red']
1
```

Accessing dictionary values by their keys is extremely efficient, even if the dictionary has many thousands of pairs.

Like lists, dictionaries are mutable: You can add or remove key:value pairs. For example:

```
>>> color = {'red' : 1, 'blue' : 2,
→ 'green' : 3}
>>> color
{'blue': 2, 'green': 3, 'red': 1}
>>> color['red'] = 0
>>> color
{'blue': 2, 'green': 3, 'red': 0}
```

Lingo Alert

Dictionaries are also referred to as *associative arrays*, *maps*, or *hash tables*.

Hashing

Python's dictionaries use a clever programming trick known as *hashing*. Essentially, each key in a dictionary is converted to a number called its *hash value* using a specially designed *hash function*. The associated values are stored in an underlying list at the index location of their hash value. Accessing a value involves converting the supplied key to a hash value and then jumping to that index location in the list. The exact details of hashing are tricky, but thankfully Python takes care of everything for us.

DICTIONARIES

Key restrictions

Dictionary keys have a couple of restrictions you need to be aware of. First, keys are *unique* within the dictionary: You can't have two key:value pairs in the same dictionary with the same key. For example:

```
>>> color = {'red' : 1, 'blue' : 2,
→ 'green' : 3,
          'red' : 4}
>>> color
{'blue': 2, 'green': 3, 'red': 4}
```

Even though we've written the key `'red'` twice, Python only stores the second pair, `'red':4`. There's simply no way to have duplicate keys: *Dictionary keys must always be unique.*

The second restriction on keys is that they must be immutable. So, for example, a dictionary key *cannot* be a list or a dictionary. The reason for this requirement is that the location in a dictionary where a key:value pair is stored depends intimately on the key. If the key changes even slightly, the location of the key:value pair in the dictionary can also change. If that happens, then pairs in the dictionary can become lost and inaccessible.

Neither of these restrictions holds for values: Values can be mutable and can appear as many times as you like within the same dictionary.

Dictionary functions

Table 7.3 lists the functions that come with all dictionaries.

As we've seen, the standard way to retrieve a value from a dictionary is to use square-bracket notation: d[key] returns the value associated with key. Calling d.get(key) will do the same thing. If you call either function when key is not in d, you'll get a KeyError.

If you are not sure whether a key is in a dictionary ahead of time, you can check by calling key in d. This expression returns True if key is in the d, and False otherwise. It is an extremely efficient check (especially as compared with using in with sequences!), so go ahead and do it when necessary.

You can also retrieve dictionary values using the pop(key) and popitem( ) functions. The difference between pop(key) and get(key) is that pop(key) returns the value associated with key and also removes its pair from the dictionary (get only returns the value). The popitem( ) function returns and removes *some* (key, value) pair from the dictionary.

Table 7.3

Dictionary Functions	
NAME	**RETURN VALUE**
d.items( )	Returns a view of the (key, value) pairs in d
d.keys( )	Returns a view of the keys of d
d.values( )	Returns a view of the values in d
d.get(key)	Returns the value associated with key
d.pop(key)	Removes key and returns its corresponding value
d.popitem( )	Returns some (key, value) pair from d
d.clear( )	Removes all items from d
d.copy( )	A copy of d
d.fromkeys(s, t)	Creates a new dictionary with keys taken from s and values taken from t
d.setdefault(key, v)	If key is in d, returns its value; if key is not in d, returns v and adds (key, v) to d
d.update(e)	Adds the (key, value) pairs in e to d; e may be another dictionary or a sequence of pairs

DICTIONARIES

You don't know ahead of time which pair will be popped, so it's useful only when you don't care about the order in which you access the dictionary elements.

The items( ), keys( ), and values( ) functions all return a special object known as a *view*. A view is linked to the original dictionary, so that if the dictionary changes, so does the view. For example:

```
>>> color
{'blue': 2, 'orange': 4, 'green': 3,
→ 'red': 0}
>>> k = color.keys( )
>>> for i in k: print(i)
blue
orange
green
red
>>> color.pop('red')
0
>>> color
{'blue': 2, 'orange': 4, 'green': 3}
>>> for i in k: print(i)
blue
orange
green
```

Sets

In Python, *sets* are collections of 0 or more items with *no duplicates*. They are similar to a dictionary that only has keys and no associated values. Sets are a good way to remove duplicates from a data collection, plus they efficiently mimic finite mathematical sets, including basic set operations such as unions and intersections.

Sets come in two categories: *mutable sets* and *immutable frozensets*. You can add and remove elements from a regular set, while a frozenset can never change once it is created.

Perhaps the most common use of sets is to remove duplicates from a sequence. For example:

```
>>> lst = [1, 1, 6, 8, 1, 5, 5, 6, 8,
→ 1, 5]
>>> s = set(lst)
>>> s
{8, 1, 5, 6}
```

Just as with dictionaries, the order of the elements in the set cannot be guaranteed.

Calling `dir(set())` in the interactive command line will list the functions that all sets come with—there are quite a few! Since sets are not as frequently used as lists and dictionaries, we won't list them all here. But keep sets in mind, and when you need them, refer to their online documentation at http://docs.python.org/dev/3.0/library/stdtypes.html#set.

Sets and Dictionaries

Sets are a relatively new addition to Python. Before sets, programmers used dictionaries to simulate sets, and indeed the first implementations of sets in Python did the same. If you find yourself using dictionaries and not caring about the values, then changing your code to use sets might make it more readable.

SETS

INPUT AND OUTPUT

To be useful, a program needs to communicate with the world around it. It needs to interact with the user, or read and write files, or access Web pages, and so on. In general, we refer to this as *input and output*, or *I/O* for short.

We've already seen basic *console I/O*, which involves printing messages and using the `input` function to read strings from the user. Now we'll see some string formatting that lets you make fancy output strings for console I/O and anywhere you need a formatted string.

Then we'll turn to *file I/O*, which is all about reading and writing files. Python provides a lot of support for basic file I/O, making it as easy as possible for programmers. In particular, we'll see how to use text files, binary files, and the powerful `pickle` module.

Formatting Strings

Python provides a number of different ways to create formatted strings. We will discuss the older string interpolation and the newer *format strings*.

String interpolation

String interpolation is a simple approach to string formatting that Python borrows from the C programming language. For instance, here's how you can control the number of decimal places in a float:

```
>>> x = 1/81
>>> print(x)
0.0123456790123
>>> print('value: %.2f' % x)
value: 0.01
>>> print('value: %.5f' % x)
value: 0.01235
```

String interpolation expressions always have the form format % values, where format is a string containing one or more occurrences of the % character. In the example 'x = %.2f' % x, the substring %.2f is a formatting command that tells Python to take the first supplied value (x) and to display it as a floating point value with two decimal places.

Table 8.1

Some Conversion Specifiers

SPECIFIER	MEANING
d	Integer
o	Octal (base 8) value
x	Lowercase hexadecimal (base 16)
X	Uppercase hexadecimal (base 16)
e	Lowercase float exponential
E	Uppercase float exponential
F	Float
s	String
%	% character

Octal and Hexadecimal

The o and x conversion specifiers, which convert values to base 8 (*octal*) and base 16 (*hexadecimal*), respectively, might seem to be of questionable value. However, in many computer-oriented applications it is convenient to represent values in base 16, or, less frequently, base 8. As we will see later in this chapter, hexadecimal is commonly used when dealing with binary files.

Conversion specifiers

The character f in the format string is a *conversion specifier*, and it tells Python how to render the corresponding value. **Table 8.1** lists the most commonly used conversion specifiers.

The e, E, and f specifiers give you different ways of representing floats. For example:

```
>>> x
0.012345679012345678
>>> print('x = %f' % x)
x = 0.012346
>>> print('x = %e' % x)
x = 1.234568e-02
>>> print('x = %E' % x)
x = 1.234568E-02
```

You can put as many specifiers as you need in a format string, although you must supply exactly one value for each specifier. For example:

```
>>> a, b, c = 'cat', 3.14, 6
>>> s = 'There\'s %d %ss older than %.2f
→ years' % (c, a, b)
>>> s
"There's 6 cats older than 3.14 years"
```

As this example shows, the format string acts as a simple template that gets filled in by the values. The values are given in a tuple, and they must be in the order in which you want them replaced.

✔ Tips

- The d, f, and s conversion specifiers are the most frequently used, so they are the ones worth remembering. In particular, f is the easiest way to control the format of floats.

- If you need the % character to appear as % itself, then you must type '%%'.

String Formatting

A second way to create fancy strings in Python is to use *format strings* with the string function `format(value, format_spec)`. For example:

```
>>> 'My {pet} has {prob}'.format(pet =
→ 'dog', prob='fleas')
'My dog has fleas'
```

In a format string, anything within curly braces is replaced. This is called *named replacement*, and it is especially readable in this example.

You can also replace values by *position*:

```
>>> 'My {0} has {1}'.format('dog',
→ 'fleas')
'My dog has fleas'
```

Or apply formatting codes similar to interpolated strings:

```
>>> '1/81 = {x}'.format(x=1/81)
'1/81 = 0.0123456790123'
>>> '1/81 = {x:f}'.format(x=1/81)
'1/81 = 0.012346'
>>> '1/81 = {x:.3f}'.format(x=1/81)
'1/81 = 0.012'
```

Templating Packages

When neither string interpolation nor format strings are powerful or flexible enough, you may want to use a templating package, such as Cheetah (www.cheetahtemplate.org), or the one that comes with Django (www.djangoproject.com). Both allow you to do some very sophisticated replacements and are good choices if you are making, say, a lot of dynamically generated Web pages.

You can specify formatting parameters *within* braces, like this:

```
>>> 'num = {x:.{d}f}'.format(x=1/81,
→ d=3)
'num = 0.012'
>>> 'num = {x:.{d}f}'.format(x=1/81,
→ d=4)
'num = 0.0123'
```

This is something you can't do with regular string interpolation.

✔ Tips

■ If you need the { or }characters to appear as themselves in a format string, type them as {{ and }}.

■ Format strings are more flexible and powerful than string interpolation, but also more complicated. If you are creating only a few simple formatted strings, string interpolation is probably the best choice. Otherwise, format strings are more useful for larger and more complex formatting jobs, such as creating Web pages or form letters for e-mail.

Reading and Writing Files

A *file* is a named collection of bits stored on a *secondary storage device*, such as a hard disk, USB drive, flash memory stick, and so on. We distinguish between two categories of files: *text files*, which are essentially strings stored on disk, and *binary files*, which are everything else.

Text files have the following characteristics:

◆ They are essentially "strings on disk." Python source code files and HTML files are examples of text files.

◆ They can be edited with any text editor. Thus, they are relatively easy for humans to read and modify.

◆ They tend to be difficult for *programs* to read. Typically, relatively complex programs called *parsers* are needed to read each different kind of text file. For instance, Python uses a special-purpose parser to help read .py files, while HTML parsers are used to read HTML files.

◆ They are usually larger than equivalent binary files. This can be a major problem when, for instance, you need to send a large text file over the Internet. Thus, text files are often compressed (for example, into *zip* format) to speed up transmission and to save disk space.

Binary files have the following characteristics:

◆ They are not usually human-readable, at least within a regular text editor. A binary file is displayed in a text editor as a random-looking series of characters. Some kinds of binary files, such as JPEG image files, have special viewers for displaying their content.

◆ They usually take up less space than equivalent text files. For instance, a binary file might group the information within it in chunks of 32 bits without using commas, spaces, or any kind of separator character.

◆ They are often easier to read and write than text files. While each binary file is different, it's often *not* necessary to write complex parsers to read them.

◆ They are often tied to a specific program and are often unusable if you lack that program. Some popular binary files may have their file formats published so that you can, if so motivated, write your programs to read and write them. However, this usually requires substantial effort.

Folders

In addition to files, *folders* (or *directories*) are used to store files and other folders. The folder structure of most file systems is quite large and complex, forming a *hierarchical folder structure*.

A *pathname* is the name used to identify a file or a folder. The *full pathname* can be quite long. For example, the Python folder on my Windows computer has this full pathname: C:\ Documents and Settings\tjd\Desktop\python.

Windows pathnames use a *backward slash* (\) character to separate names in a path, and they start with the letter of the disk drive (in this example, *C:*).

On Mac and Linux systems, a *forward slash* (/) is used to separate names. Plus, there is no drive letter at the start. For example, here is the full pathname for my Python folder on Linux: /home/tjd/Desktop/python.

✔ Tips

- Recall that if you want to write a \ character in a Python string, it must be doubled:

  `'C:\\home\\tjd\\Desktop\\python'`

  To avoid the double backslashes, you can use a *raw string*:

  `r'C:\home\tjd\Desktop\python'`

- Getting Python programs to work with both styles of pathnames is a bit tricky, and you should read the documentation for Python's os.path module for (much!) more information.

The current working directory

Many programs use the idea of a *current working directory*, or *cwd*. This is simply one directory that has been designated as the *default directory*. Whenever you do something to a file or a folder without providing a full pathname, Python assumes you mean a file or a folder in the current working directory.

Examining Files and Folders

Python provides many functions that return information about your computer's files and folders (its *file system*). **Table 8.2** lists a few of the most useful ones.

Let's write a couple of useful functions to see how these work. For instance, a common task is retrieving the files and folders in the current working directory. Writing os.listdir(os.getcwd()) is unwieldy, so we can write this function:

```
# list.py
def list_cwd():
    return os.listdir(os.getcwd())
```

The following two related helper functions use list comprehensions to return just the files and folders in the current working directory:

```
# list.py
def files_cwd():
    return [p for p in list_cwd()
            if os.path.isfile(p)]

def folders_cwd():
    return [p for p in list_cwd()
            if os.path.isdir(p)]
```

Table 8.2

Useful File and Folder Functions	
NAME	ACTION
os.getcwd()	Returns the name of the current working directory
os.listdir(p)	Returns a list of strings of the names of all the files and folders in the folder specified by path p
os.chdir(p)	Sets the current working directory to be path p
os.path.isfile(p)	Returns True just when path p specifies the name of a file, and False otherwise
os.path.isdir(p)	Returns True just when path p specifies the name of a folder, and False otherwise
os.stat(fname)	Returns information about fname, such as its size in bytes and the last modification time

If you just want a list of, say, the `.py` files in the current working directory, then this will work:

```
# list.py
def list_py(path = None):
    if path == None:
        path = os.getcwd()
    return [fname for fname in
    ➝os.listdir(path)
            if os.path.isfile(fname)
            if fname.endswith('.py')]
```

This function plays a useful trick with its input parameter: If you call `list_py()` without a parameter, it runs on the current working directory. Otherwise, it runs on the directory you pass in.

Finally, here's a function that returns the sum of the sizes of the files in the current working directory:

```
# list.py
def size_in_bytes(fname):
    return os.stat(fname).st_size

def cwd_size_in_bytes():
    total = 0
    for name in files_cwd():
        total = total + size_in_
        ➝bytes(name)
    return total
```

A Neat Trick

The `cwd_size_in_bytes` function can be written as a single-line function:

```
def cwd_size_in_bytes2():
  return sum(size_in_bytes(f)
             for f in files_cwd())
```

The details of how `cwd_size_in_bytes2` works is beyond the scope of an introductory book, but if you are curious about this more compact form, search the Web for *python generator expressions*.

✔ Tips

■ To save space, we've removed the doc strings for these functions. However, the supplementary code files on Google's "pythonintro" Web site (http://pythonintro.googlecode.com) all include doc strings.

■ You can tell from the name `cwd_size_in_bytes` that the return value will be in bytes. Putting the unit of the return value in the function name prevents the need to check the documentation for the units.

■ In general, it's a good idea to use lots of functions. Even single-line functions such as `list_dir()` are useful because they make your programs easier to read and maintain.

■ The `os.stat()` function is fairly complex and provides much more information about files than we've shown here. Check Python's online documentation for more information (http://docs.python.org/dev/3.0/library/os.html).

Processing Text Files

Python makes it relatively easy to process text files. In general, file processing follows the three steps shown in **Figure 8.1**.

Reading a text file, line by line

Perhaps the most common way of reading a text file is to read it one line at a time. For example, this prints the contents of a file to the screen:

```python
# printfile.py
def print_file1(fname):
    f = open(fname, 'r')
    for line in f:
        print(line, end = '')
    f.close()  # optional
```

The first line of the function opens the file: open requires the name of the file you want to process, and also the *mode* you want it opened in. We are only reading the file, so we open the file in read mode 'r'. **Table 8.3** lists Python's main file modes.

The open function returns a special *file object*, which represents the file on disk. Importantly, open does *not* read the file into RAM. Instead, in this example, the file is read a line at a time using a for-loop.

The last line of print_file1 closes the file. As the comment notes, this is optional: Python *almost always* automatically closes files for you. In this case, variable f is local to print_file1, so when print_file1 ends, Python automatically closes and then deletes the file object (not the *file* itself, of course!) that f points to.

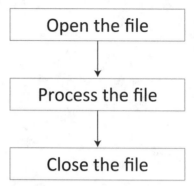

Figure 8.1 The three main steps for processing a text file. A file must be opened before you can use it, and then it should be closed when you are done with it to ensure that all changes are committed to the file.

Table 8.3

Python File Modes	
CHARACTER	MEANING
'r'	Open for reading (default)
'w'	Open for writing
'a'	Open for appending to the end of the file
'b'	Binary mode
't'	Text mode (default)
'+'	Open a file for reading and writing

✔ Tips

■ The `print` statement in `print_file1` sets `end = ''` because the lines of a file always end with a \n character. Thus if we had written just `print(line)`, the file would be displayed with extra blank lines (try it and see!).

■ If errors occur while a file is open, it is possible that the program could end without the file being properly closed. In the next chapter, we will see how to handle such errors and ensure that a file is always correctly closed.

Reading a text file as a string

Another common way of reading a text file is to read it as one big string. For example:

```
# printfile.py
def print_file2(fname):
    f = open(fname, 'r')
    print(f.read())
    f.close()
```

This is shorter and simpler than `print_file1`, so many programmers prefer it. However, if the file you are reading is *very* large, it will take up a lot of RAM, which could slow down, or even crash, your computer.

Finally, we note that many programmers would write this function with a single-line body:

```
# printfile.py
def print_file3(fname):
    print(open(fname, 'r').read())
```

While this more compact form might take some getting used to, many programmers like this style because it is both quick to type and still relatively readable.

Reading by Default

When reading a text file, you can use `open` with just the filename. For example:

```
f = open(fname)
```

When no mode parameters are supplied, Python assumes you are opening a text file for reading.

Writing to a text file

Writing text files is only a little more involved than reading them. For example, this function creates a new text file named `story.txt`:

```
# write.py
def make_story1():
    f = open('story.txt', 'w')
    f.write('Mary had a little lamb,\n')
    f.write('and then she had some
    → more.\n')
```

The `'w'` tells Python to open the file in *write mode*. To put text into the file, you call `f.write` with the string you want to put into the file. Strings are written to the file in the order in which they are given.

Important: If `story.txt` already exists, then calling `open('story.txt', 'w')` will *delete it!* If you want to avoid overwriting `story.txt`, you need to check to see if it exists:

```
# write.py
import os
def make_story2():
    if os.path.isfile('story.txt'):
        print('story.txt already exists)
    else:
        f = open('story.txt', 'w')
        f.write('Mary had a little
        → lamb,\n')
        f.write('and then she had some
        → more.\n')
```

Appending to a text file

One common way of adding strings to a text file is to append them to the end of the file. Unlike `'w'` mode, this does *not* delete anything that might already be in the file. For example:

```
def add_to_story(line,
                 fname = 'story.txt'):
    f = open(fname, 'a')
    f.write(line)
```

The important thing to note here is that the file is opened in append mode `'a'`.

Inserting a string at the start of a file

Writing a string to the *beginning* of a file is not as easy as appending one to the end because the Windows, Linux, and Macintosh operating systems don't directly support inserting text at the beginning of a text file. Perhaps the simplest way to insert text at the beginning of a file is to read the file into a string, insert the new text into the string, and then write the string back to the original file. For example:

```
def insert_title(title,
                 fname = 'story.txt'):
    f = open(fname, 'r+')

    temp = f.read()
    temp = title + '\n\n' + temp

    f.seek(0)  # reset file pointer
               # to beginning
    f.write(temp)
```

First, notice that we open the file using the special mode 'r+', which means the file can be both read from and written to. Then we read the entire file into the string temp and insert the title using string concatenation.

Before writing the newly created string back into the file, we first have to tell the file object f to reset its internal *file pointer*. All text file objects keep track of where they are in the file, and after f.read() is called, the file pointer is at the very end. Calling f.seek(0) puts it back at the start of the file, so that when we write to f, it begins at the start of the file.

Processing Binary Files

If a file is not a text file, then it is considered to be a binary file. Binary files are opened in 'b' mode, and you access the individual bytes of the file. For example:

```python
def is_gif(fname):
    f = open(fname, 'br')
    first4 = tuple(f.read(4))
    return first4 == (0x47, 0x49, 0x46,
                      0x38)
```

This function tests if fname is a GIF image file by checking to see if its first 4 bytes are (0x47, 0x49, 0x46, 0x38) (all GIFs must start with those 4 bytes).

In Python, numbers like 0x47 are base-16 *hexadecimal numbers*, or *hex* for short. They are very convenient for dealing with bytes, since each hexadecimal digit corresponds to a pattern of 4 bits, and so 1 byte can be described using two hex digits (such as 0x47).

Notice that the file is opened in 'br' mode, which means *binary reading* mode. When reading a binary file, you call f.read(n), which reads the next n bytes. As with text files, binary file objects use a file pointer to keep track of which byte should be read next in the file.

Pickling

Accessing the individual bytes of binary files is a very low-level operation that, while useful in *systems programming*, is less useful in higher-level *applications programming*.

Pickling is often a much more convenient way to deal with binary files. Python's `pickle` module lets you easily read and write almost any data structure. For example:

```
# picklefile.py
import pickle

def make_pickled_file():
    grades = {'alan' : [4, 8, 10, 10],
              'tom' : [7, 7, 7, 8],
              'dan' : [5, None, 7, 7],
              'may' : [10, 8, 10, 10]}

    outfile = open('grades.dat', 'wb')
    pickle.dump(grades, outfile)

def get_pickled_data():
    infile = open('grades.dat', 'rb')
    grades = pickle.load(infile)
    return grades
```

Essentially, pickling lets you store a data structure on disk using `pickle.dump` and then retrieve it later with `pickle.load`. This is an extremely useful feature in many application programs, so you should keep it in mind whenever you need to store binary data.

PROCESSING BINARY FILES

Lingo Alert

The Python pickle module performs what is generally known as *object serialization*, or just *serialization*. The idea is to take a complex data structure and convert it to a stream of bytes—that is, create a serial representation of the data structure.

✔ Tips

■ In addition to data structures, pickling can store functions.

■ You can't use pickling to read or write binary files that have a specific format, such as GIF files. For such files, you must work byte by byte.

■ Python has a module called shelve that provides an even higher-level way to store and retrieve data. The shelve module essentially lets you treat a file as if it were a dictionary. For more details, see the Python documentation (http://docs. python.org/dev/3.0/library/shelve.html).

■ Python also has a module named sqlite3, which provides an interface to the sqlite database. This lets you write SQL commands to store and retrieve data very much like using a larger database product such as Postgres or MySQL. For more details, see the Python documenta- tion (http://docs.python.org/dev/3.0/ library/sqlite3.html).

Reading Web Pages

Python has good support for accessing the Web. One common task is to have a program automatically read a Web page. This is easily done using the `urllib` module:

```
>>> import urllib.request
>>> resp = urllib.request.
→ urlopen('http://www.python.org')
>>> html = resp.read()
>>> html[:25]
b'<!DOCTYPE html PUBLIC "-/'
```

Now `html` contains the complete text of the Web page at www.python.org. It is in HTML, of course, so it looks just like what you would see if you were to use the View Source option on your Web browser. Since the Web page is now a string on your computer, you can use Python's string-manipulation functions to extract information from it.

✔ Tips

■ The `urllib` module also lets you programmatically post information to Web forms. For details of how to do this and more, see the Python documentation (http://docs. python.org/dev/3.0/howto/urllib2.html).

■ Reading a Web page into a string is the first step in creating a Web browser. The next major step is to parse the string—to identify and extract titles, paragraphs, tables, and so on. Python provides a basic HTML parsing library in the `html.parser` module. See the Python documentation (http://docs.python.org/dev/3.0/library/html.parser.html) for details.

continues on next page

■ Another nifty module is `webbrowser`, which lets you programmatically display a Web page in a browser. For example, when you type this into Python, the Yahoo! Home page should pop up in your default Web browser:

```
>>> import webbrowser
>>> webbrowser.open
→ ('http://www.yahoo.com')
True

>>>
```

EXCEPTION HANDLING

Exceptions are a solution to a difficult problem: How can programs deal with *unexpected errors*? For instance, what happens if a file disappears in the middle of being read because some other program on your computer has deleted it? Or what if the Web site your program is downloading pages from suddenly crashes?

In these and many other situations, what Python does is *raise an exception*. An exception is a special kind of error object that you can *catch* and then examine in order to determine how to handle the *error*.

Exceptions can change the flow of control of your program. Depending on when it occurs, an exception can cause the flow of control to jump out of the middle of a function or loop into another block of code that does error handling.

Often, you cannot be sure exactly which line might raise an exception, and this creates some tricky problems. Thus Python provides special exception-handling constructs for both catching exceptions and executing *clean-up code* whether or not an exception is raised.

Exceptions

An example of an exception is IOError, which is raised when you try to open a file that doesn't exist:

```
>>> open('unicorn.dat')
Traceback (most recent call last):
  File "<pyshell#1>", line 1, in
  → <module>
    open('unicorn.dat')
  File "C:\Python30\lib\io.py", line
  → 284, in __new__
    return open(*args, **kwargs)
  File "C:\Python30\lib\io.py", line
  → 223, in open
    closefd)
IOError: [Errno 2] No such file or
→ directory: 'unicorn.dat'
```

When an exception is raised and is not caught or handled in any way, Python immediately halts the program and outputs a *traceback*, which is a list of the functions that were called before the exception occurred. This can be quite useful in pinning down exactly what line causes an error.

The last line of the traceback indicates that an IOError exception has been raised, and, specifically, it means that unicorn.dat could not be found in the current working directory. The error message given by an IOError differs depending on the exact reason for the exception.

Lingo Alert

In Python, when an exception occurs, we say that it has been *raised*, or has been *thrown*. If we do nothing with a raised exception, the program usually halts immediately with a *traceback*, or a *stack trace*. However, especially in programs meant to be used by other people, we usually *catch* and *handle* exceptions, as we will see shortly.

Raising an exception

As we saw with the open function, Python's built-in functions and library functions usually raise exceptions when something unexpected happens.

For instance, dividing by zero throws an exception:

```
>>> 1/0
Traceback (most recent call last):
  File "<pyshell#0>", line 1, in
 → <module>
    1/0
ZeroDivisionError: int division or
 → modulo by zero
```

Syntax errors can also cause exceptions in Python:

```
>>> x := 5
SyntaxError: invalid syntax
 → (<pyshell#2>, line 1)
>>> print('hello world)

SyntaxError: EOL while scanning string
 → literal (<pyshell#3>, line 1)
```

You can also intentionally raise an exception anywhere in your code using the raise statement. For example:

```
>>> raise IOError('This is a test!')
Traceback (most recent call last):
  File "<pyshell#6>", line 1, in
 → <module>
    raise IOError('This is a test!')
IOError: This is a test!
```

Python has numerous built-in exceptions organized into a hierarchy: See the Python documentation (http://docs.python.org/dev/3.0/library/exceptions.html#bltin-exceptions) for more details.

Catching Exceptions

You have essentially two options for dealing with a raised exception:

1. Ignore the exception and let your program crash with a traceback. This is usually what you want when you are developing a program, since the traceback provides helpful debugging information.

2. Catch the exception and print a friendly error message, or possibly even try to fix the problem. This is almost always what you want to do with a program meant to be used by non-programmers: Regular users don't want to deal with tracebacks!

Here's an example of how to catch an exception. Suppose you want to read an integer from the user, prompting repeatedly until a valid integer is entered:

```
def get_age():
    while True:
        try:
            n = int(input('How old are
            ↪ you? '))
            return n
        except ValueError:
            print('Please enter an
            ↪ integer value.')
```

Inside this function's while-loop is a *try/ except block*. You put whatever code you like in the try part of the block, with the understanding that one or more lines of that code *might* raise an exception.

If any line of the try block does raise an exception, then the flow of control immediately jumps to the except block, skipping over any statements that have not been executed yet. In this example, the return statement will be skipped when an exception is raised.

What Exceptions Do Functions Raise?

How do we know to check for an exception named ValueError in get_age()? The answer depends on the function's documentation. A well-documented function will tell you what exceptions it might raise. For instance, the documentation for the open function (http://docs. python.org/dev/3.0/library/functions. html?#open) tells you that it might raise an IOError. However, not all of Python's built-in functions are so forthcoming: The documentation for the int function says nothing about what exceptions it might raise. In this case, you have to figure out the possible exceptions by reading samples of other Python code, or by doing command-line experiments.

If the try block raises no exceptions, then the except ValueError block is ignored and not executed.

So in this example, the int() function raises a ValueError if the user enters a string that is not a valid integer. When that happens, the flow of control jumps to the except ValueError block and prints the error message. When a ValueError is raised, the return statement is skipped—the flow of control jumps immediately to the except block.

If the user enters a valid integer, then no exception is raised, and Python proceeds to the following return statement, thus ending the function.

Try/except blocks

Try/except blocks work a little bit like if-statements. However, they are different in an important way: If-statements decide what to do based on the evaluation of Boolean expressions, while try/except blocks decide what to do based on whether or not an exception is raised.

A function can raise more than one kind of exception, and it can even raise the same type of exception for different reasons. Look at these three different int() exceptions (the tracebacks have been trimmed for readability):

```
>>> int('two')
ValueError: invalid literal for int()
→ with base 10: 'two'
>>> int(2, 10)
TypeError: int() can't convert
→ non-string with explicit base
>>> int('2', 1)
ValueError: int() arg 2 must be >= 2
→ and <= 36
```

So int() raises ValueError for at least two different reasons, while it raises TypeError in at least one other case.

CATCHING EXCEPTIONS

Catching multiple exceptions

You can write try/except blocks to handle multiple exceptions. For example, you can group together multiple exceptions in the except clause:

```
def convert_to_int1(s, base):
    try:
        return int(s, base)
    except (ValueError, TypeError):
        return 'error'
```

Or, if you care about the specific exception that is thrown, you can add extra except clauses:

```
def convert_to_int2(s, base):
    try:
        return int(s, base)
    except ValueError:
        return 'value error'
    except TypeError:
        return 'type error'
```

Catching any exception

If you write an except clause without any exception name, it will catch any and all exceptions:

```
def convert_to_int3(s, base):
    try:
        return int(s, base)
    except:
        return 'error'
```

This form of except clause will catch any exception—it doesn't care about what kind of error has occurred, just that one has occurred. In many situations, this is all you need.

Clean-Up Actions

A `finally` code block can be added to any try/except block to perform clean-up actions. For example:

```
def invert(x):
    try:
        return 1 / x
    except ZeroDivisionError:
        return 'error'
    finally:
        print('invert(%s) done' % x)
```

The code block underneath `finally` will always be executed after the `try` block or the `except` block. This is quite useful when you have code that you want to perform regardless of whether an exception is raised. For instance, file close statements are often put in `finally` clauses so that files are guaranteed to be closed, even if an unexpected `IOError` occurs.

The with statement

Python's `with` statement is another way to ensure that clean-up actions (such as closing a file) are done as soon as possible, even if there is an exception. For example, consider this code, which prints a file to the screen with numbers for each line:

```
num = 1
f = open(fname)
for line in f:
    print('%04d %s' % (num, line),
          end = '')
    num = num + 1
    # following code
```

What's unknown here is *when* the file object f is closed. At some point *after* the for-loop, f will usually be closed. But we don't know when precisely that will happen: It will remain unclosed but unused for an indeterminate amount of time, which might be a problem if other programs try to access the file.

To ensure that the file is closed as soon as it is no longer needed, use a `with` statement:

```
num = 1
  with open(fname, 'r') as f:
    for line in f:
        print('%04d %s' % (num, line),
        → end = '')
        num = num + 1
```

The onscreen results are the same as the previous code, but when you use a `with` statement, the file objects' clean-up action (that is to say, closing the file) is automatically called as soon as the for-loop ends. Thus f does not sit around unclosed.

Alternative Formatting

The `print` statements in these two snippets of code use string interpolation to print a right-justified and zero-padded number before each line of the printed file. If you prefer string formatting, you could replace the `print` statements with this one:

```
print('{0:04} {1}'.format(num,
                          line),
    end = '')
```

OBJECT-ORIENTED PROGRAMMING

In this chapter, we will briefly look at *object-oriented programming*, or *OOP* for short. OOP is a methodology for organizing programs that encourages careful design and code reuse. Most modern programming languages support it, and it is has proved to be a practical way to structure and create large programs.

We've already been using objects in Python; numbers, strings, lists, dictionaries, files, and functions are all examples of objects.

To create new kinds of objects, you must first create a *class*. A class is essentially a blueprint for creating an object of a particular kind. The class specifies what data and functions the objects will contain, and how they relate to other classes. An object *encapsulates* both the data and functions that operate on that data.

An important OOP feature is *inheritance*: You can create new classes that inherit their data and functions from an existing class. When used properly, inheritance can save you from rewriting code, and it can also make your programs easier to understand.

Finally, *polymorphism* is a consequence of some OOP designs that can save you from writing unnecessary code. Essentially, polymorphic code does not know exactly what functions it will be calling until it receives the objects passed to it while the program is running.

Writing a Class

Let's jump right into OOP by creating a
simple class to represent a person:

```
# person.py
class Person:
    """ Class to represent a person
    """
    def __init__(self):
        self.name = ''
        self.age = 0
```

This defines a *class* named Person: It defines
the data and functions a Person object will
contain. We've started simple and defined a
Person to have a name and an age; we haven't
(yet) given Person any functions except for
__init__, which is the standard function for
initializing an object's values. As we will see,
Python automatically calls __init__ when
you create a Person object.

A function defined inside a class is called a
method. Just like __init__, methods must
have self as their first parameter (self will
be discussed in more detail shortly).

To create Person objects, we can do this:

```
>>> p = Person()
>>> p
<__main__.Person object at 0x00AC3370>
>>> p.age
0
>>> p.name
''
>>> p.age = 55
>>> p.age
55
>>> p.name = 'Moe'
>>> p.name
'Moe'
```

Lingo Alert

In some OOP languages, __init__ is
called a *constructor*, because it constructs
the object. A constructor is called every
time a new object is created. In languages
such as Java and C++, an explicit new keyword is used to indicate when an object is
being constructed.

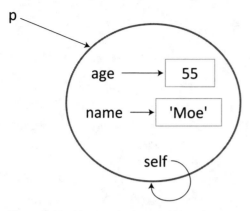

p

age → 55

name → 'Moe'

self

Figure 10.1 In this example, the variable p points to a Person object (represented by the circle). As we know from looking at the Person class, a Person object contains an age and a name. These can be used just like regular variables, with the stipulation that they be accessed using dot notation—that is, p.age and p.name. The special variable self is automatically added by Python to all objects; it points to the object itself and lets functions within the class unambiguously refer to the data and functions within the object.

To create a Person object, we simply call Person( ). This causes Python to run the _ _init_ _ function in the Person class and to return a new object of type Person.

The age and name variables are inside an object, and every newly created Person object has its own personal copy of age and name. Thus, if you want to access age or name, you must specify what object holds them using *dot notation*.

The self parameter

You'll notice that we don't provide any parameters for Person(), but the _ _init_ _ (self) function expects an input named self. That's because in OOP, self is a variable that *refers to the object itself* (**Figure 10.1**). This is a simple idea, but one that trips up many beginners.

✔ Tips

- All classes should have an _ _init_ _ (self) method whose job is to initialize the object—for example, initializing an object's variables. The _ _init_ _ method is only called once when the object is created. As we will see, you can provide extra parameters to _ _init_ _ if needed.

- We have followed standard Python terminology and given the first parameter of _ _init_ _ the name self. This name is not required: You can use any variable name you like instead of self. However, the use of self is a universal convention in Python, and using any other name would likely just cause confusion for any programmer trying to read your code. Some other languages, such as Java and C++, use—and require—the name this.

- Objects can be used like any other data type in Python: You can pass them to functions, store them in lists and dictionaries, pickle them in files, and so on.

Displaying Objects

As mentioned, a method is simply a function defined within an object. Let's add a method to the Person class that prints the contents of a Person object:

```
# person.py
class Person:
    """ Class to represent a person
    """
    def __init__(self):
        self.name = ''
        self.age = 0

    def display(self):
        print("Person('%s', age)" %
        → (self.name, self.age))
```

The display method prints the contents of a Person object to the screen in a format useful to a programmer:

```
>>> p = Person()
>>> p.display()
Person('', 0)
>>> p.name = 'Bob'
>>> p.age = 25
>>> p.display()
Person('Bob', 25)
```

The display method works fine, but we can do better: Python provides some special functions that let you customize objects for seamless printing. For instance, the special __str__ method is used to generate a string representation of an object:

```
# person.py
class Person:
    # __init__ method removed for space
    def display(self):
        print("Person('%s', age)" %
        → (self.name, self.age))

    def __str__(self):
        return "Person('%s', age)"
        → % (self.name, self.age)
```

Now we can write code like this:

```
>>> p = Person()
>>> str(p)
"Person('', 0)"
```

We can use str to simplify the display method:

```
# person.py

class Person:

    # __init__ method removed for space
    def display(self):
        print(str(self))

    def __str__(self):
        return "Person('%s', age)" %
        → (self.name, self.age)
```

You can also define a special method named __repr__ that returns the "official" representation of an object. For example, the default representation of a Person is not very helpful:

```
>>> p = Person()
>>> p
<__main__.Person object at 0x012C3170>
```

By adding a __repr__ method, we can control the string that is printed here. In most objects, it is the same as the __str__ method:

```
# person.py
class Person:
    # __init__ method removed for space
    def display(self):
        print(str(self))

    def __str__(self):
        return "Person('%s', age)" %
        → (self.name, self.age)

    def __repr__(self):
        return str(self)
```

Now `Person` objects are easier to work with:

```
>>> p = Person()
>>> p
Person('', 0)
>>> str(p)
"Person('', 0)"
```

✔ Tips

- When creating your own classes and objects, it is almost always worthwhile to write `__str__` and `__repr__` functions. They are extremely useful for displaying the contents of your objects, which is helpful when debugging your programs.

- If you define a `__repr__` method but not a `__str__` method, then when you call `str()` on the object, it will run `__repr__`.

- Once you've added the `__repr__` method, the display method for `Person` can be further simplified:

```
def display(self):
    print(self)
```

In practice, it's often not necessary to write a `display` method.

- The Python documentation recommends that the string representation of an object be the same as the code you would write to create that object. This is a very useful convention: It lets you easily re-create objects by cutting and pasting the string representation into the command line.

Flexible Initialization

If you want to create a Person object with a particular name and age, you must currently do this:

```
>>> p = Person()
>>> p.name = 'Moe'
>>> p.age = 55
>>> p
Person('Moe', 55)
```

A more convenient approach is to pass the name and age to `__init__` when the object is constructed. So let's rewrite `__init__` to allow for this:

```
# person.py
class Person:
    def __init__(self, name = '',
                       age = 0):
        self.name = name
        self.age = age
```

Now initializing a Person is much simpler:

```
>>> p = Person('Moe', 55)
>>> p
Person('Moe', 55)
```

Since the parameters to `__init__` have default values, you can even create an "empty" Person:

```
>>> p = Person()
>>> p
Person('', 0)
```

Notice inside the `__init__` method that we use `self.name` and `name` (and also `self.age` and `age`). The variable `name` refers to the value passed into `__init__`, while `self.name` refers to the value stored in the object. The use of `self` helps make clear which is which.

✔ Tip

- While it is easy to create default values for `__init__` parameters and thus allow the creation of empty (or *null*) Person objects, it is not so clear if this is a good idea from a design point of view. An empty Person does not have a real name or age, so you will need to check for that in code that processes Person objects. Constantly checking for special cases can soon become a real burden, and forgetting to do it is easy . Thus, many programmers prefer not to give the `__init__` parameters default values in this case, and to avoid empty objects altogether.

Setters and Getters

As it stands now, we can both read and write the *name* and *age* values of a Person object using dot notation:

```
>>> p = Person('Moe', 55)
>>> p.age
55
>>> p.name
'Moe'
>>> p.name = 'Joe'
>>> p.name
'Joe'
>>> p
Person('Joe', 55)
```

A problem with this is that we could, accidentally, set the age to be a nonsensical value, such as -45 or 509. With regular Python variables there is no way to restrict what values they can be assigned. However, within an object, we can write special *setter* and *getter* methods that give us control over how values are accessed.

First, let's add a setter method that changes *age* only if a sensible value is given:

```
def set_age(self, age):
    if 0 < age <= 150:
        self.age = age
```

Now we can write code like this:

```
>>> p = Person('Jen', 25)
>>> p
Person('Jen', 25)
>>> p.set_age(30)
>>> p
Person('Jen', 30)
>>> p.set_age(-6)
>>> p
Person('Jen', 30)
```

One common complaint about this kind of setter is that typing p.set_age(30) is more cumbersome than p.age = 30.

Property decorators

Property *decorators* combine the brevity of variable assignment with the flexibility of setter and getter functions. Decorators indicate that a function or method is special in some way, and here we use them to indicate which methods are setters and getters.

A getter returns the value of a variable, and we indicate this using the `@property` decorator:

```
@property
def age(self):
    """ Returns this person's age.
    """
    return self._age
```

You can see here that we've created a method called `age` that takes no parameters (other than the required `self`). We've put `@property` before it to indicate that it's a getter; the name of the method is `age`, and that's the name we will use to set the variable.

We have also renamed the underlying `self.age` variable to `self._age`. Putting an underscore in front of an object variable is a common convention, and we use it here to distinguish it from the `age` method we just created. You need to replace every occurrence of `self.age` in `Person` with `self._age`.

Decorators

Decorators are a general-purpose construct in Python used to systematically modify existing functions. They are usually placed at the beginning of a function, and start with a @ character. We will use them in this book for this one example of creating setters and getters.

For consistency, it is also a good idea to everywhere replace self.name with self._name. The modified Person class should look like this:

```
# person.py
class Person:
    def __init__(self, name = '',
                       age = 0):
        self._name = name
        self._age = age

    @property
    def age(self):
        return self._age

    def set_age(self, age):
        if 0 < age <= 150:
            self._age = age

    def display(self):
        print(self)

    def __str__(self):
        return "Person('%s', %s)" %
→ (self._name, self._age)

    def __repr__(self):
        return str(self)
```

To create an age setter, we rename the set_age method to age and decorate it with @age.setter:

```
@age.setter
def age(self, age):
    if 0 < age <= 150:
        self._age = age
```

With these changes, we can now write code like this:

```
>>> p = Person('Lia', 33)
>>> p
Person('Lia', 33)
>>> p.age = 55
>>> p.age
55
>>> p.age = -4
>>> p.age
55
```

continues on next page

The setter and getters for `age` work just as if we were using the variable `age` directly. The difference is that now when you call, say, `p.age = -4`, Python is really calling the `age(self, age)` method. Similarly, when you write `p.age`, the `age(self)` method is called. Thus we get the advantage of the simple assignment syntax combined with the flexibility of controlling how variables are set and get.

Private variables

You can sneak in illegal changes by accessing `self._age` directly:

```
>>> p._age = -44
>>> p
Person('Lia', -44)
```

One way to decrease the chance of this kind of problem is to rename `self._age` to `self.__age`—that is to say, to put two underscores in front of the variable name. The two underscores declare that `age` is a *private* variable that is not meant to be accessed by any code outside of `Person`. To access `self.__age` directly, you now have to put `_Person` on the front like this:

```
>>> p._Person__age = -44
>>> p
Person('Lia', -44)
```

While this does not prevent you from modifying internal variables, it does make it almost impossible to do so accidentally.

Lingo Alert

Variables that don't begin with an underscore are called *public* variables, and any code can access them.

✔ Tips

- When writing large programs, a useful rule of thumb is to always make object variables private (that is, starting with two underscores) by default, and then change them to be public if you have a good reason to do so. This way, you will prevent errors caused by unintended meddling with the internals of an object.

- The syntax for creating setters and getters is strange at first, but once you get used to it, it is fairly clear. Keep in mind that you don't always need to create special setters and getters; for simple objects, like the original Person, regular variables may be fine.

- Some programmers prefer to avoid setters whenever possible, thus making the object immutable (just like numbers, strings, and tuples). In an object with no setters, after you create the object, there is no "official" way to change anything within it. As with other immutable objects, this can prevent many subtle errors and allow different variables to share the same object (thus saving memory). The downside is, of course, that if you do need to modify the object, your only option is to create a new object that incorporates the change.

- If the programmer tries to set the age to be something out of range, then age(self, age) doesn't make any change. An alternative approach is to purposely raise an exception, thus requiring any code that calls it to handle the exception. The advantage of raising an exception is that it might help you find more errors: Trying to set the age to be a nonsensical value is likely a sign of a problem elsewhere in your program.

Inheritance

Inheritance is a mechanism for reusing classes. Essentially, inheritance allows you to create a brand new class by adding extra variables and methods to a copy of an existing class.

Suppose we are creating a game that has human players and computer players. Let's create a `Player` class that contains things common to all players, such as the score and a name:

```python
# players.py
class Player:
    def __init__(self, name):
        self._name = name
        self._score = 0

    def reset_score(self):
        self._score = 0

    def incr_score(self):
        self._score = self._score + 1

    def get_name(self):
        return self._name

    def __str__(self):
        return "name = '%s', score = %s"
        → % (self._name, self._score)

    def __repr__(self):
        return 'Player(%s)' % str(self)
```

We can create and use `Player` objects this way:

```python
>>> p = Player('Moe')
>>> p
Player(name = 'Moe', score = 0)
>>> p.incr_score()
>>> p
Player(name = 'Moe', score = 1)
>>> p.reset_score()
>>> p
Player(name = 'Moe', score = 0)
```

Let's assume there are two kinds of players: humans and computers. The main difference is that humans enter their moves from the keyboard, while computers generate their moves from functions. Otherwise they are the same, each having a name and a score as in the `Player` class.

So let's write a `Human` class that represents a `Human` player. The simplest way to do that would be to cut and paste a new copy of the `Player` class, and then add a `make_move(self)` method that asks the player to make a move. While that approach certainly would work, a much better way is to use *inheritance*. We can define the `Human` class to *inherit* all the variables and methods from the `Player` class so that we don't have to rewrite them:

```
class Human(Player):
    pass
```

In Python, the `pass` statement means "Do nothing." This is a complete—and useful!—definition for the `Human` class. It simply inherits the code from `Player`, which lets us do the following:

```
>>> h = Human('Jerry')
>>> h
Player(name = 'Jerry', score = 0)
>>> h.incr_score()
>>> h
Player(name = 'Jerry', score = 1)
>>> h.reset_score()
>>> h
Player(name = 'Jerry', score = 0)
```

This is pretty impressive given that we wrote only two lines of code for the `Human` class!

Lingo Alert

Many different terms are used to describe inheritance. Given that class `Human` inherits from class `Player`, we can say the following:

◆ Human *extends* Player.

◆ Human is *derived* from Player.

◆ Human is a *subclass* of Player, and Player is a *superclass* of Human.

◆ Human *isa* Player.

The last term, *isa*, implies that all humans are players. Thinking about possible isa relationships between classes is one way to create class hierarchies.

Overriding methods

One small wart is that the string representation of h says Player when it would be more accurate for it to say Human. We can fix that by giving Human its own _ _repr_ _ method:

```
class Human(Player):
    def __repr__(self):
        return 'Human(%s)' % str(self)
```

Now we get this:

```
>>> h = Human('Jerry')
>>> h
Human(name = 'Jerry', score = 0)
```

This is an example of *method overriding*: The _ _repr_ _ method in Human overrides the _ _repr_ _ method inherited from Player. This is a common way to customize inherited classes.

Now it's easy to write a similar Computer class to represent computer moves:

```
class Computer(Player):
    def __repr__(self):
        return Computer(%s)' % str(self)
```

These three classes form a small *class hierarchy*, as shown in the *class diagram* of **Figure 10.2**. The Player class is called the *base* class, and the other two classes are *derived*, or *extended*, classes.

Essentially, an extended class inherits the variables and methods from the base class. Any code you want to be shared by all the derived classes should be placed inside the base class.

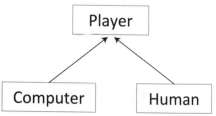

Figure 10.2 A class diagram showing how the Player, Human, and Computer classes relate. The arrows indicate inheritance, and the entire diagram is a hierarchy of classes. The more abstract (that is, general) classes appear near the top, and the more concrete (that is, specific) ones nearer the bottom.

Lingo Alert

It's also common to use the term *parent class* to refer to the base class and *child class* to refer to the derived class.

INHERITANCE

Polymorphism

To demonstrate the power of OOP, let's implement a simple game called *Undercut*. In Undercut, two players simultaneously pick an integer from 1 to 10 (inclusive). If a player picks a number one less than the other player—if he undercuts the other player by 1—then he wins. Otherwise, the game is a draw. For example, if Thomas and Bonnie are playing Undercut, and they pick the numbers 9 and 10, respectively, then Thomas wins. If, instead, they choose 4 and 7, the game is a draw.

Here's a function for playing one game of Undercut:

```
def play_undercut(p1, p2):
    p1.reset_score()
    p2.reset_score()
    m1 = p1.get_move()
    m2 = p2.get_move()
    print("%s move: %s" % (p1.get_name(),
                               m1))
    print("%s move: %s" % (p2.get_name(),
                               m2))
    if m1 == m2 - 1:
        p1.incr_score()
        return p1, p2,
            '%s wins!' % p1.get_name()
    elif m2 == m1 - 1:
        p2.incr_score()
        return p1, p2,
            '%s wins!' % p2.get_name()
    else:
        return p1, p2, 'draw: no winner'
```

If you read this function carefully, you will note that `p1.get_move()` and `p2.get_move()` are called. We haven't yet implemented these functions because they are game-dependent. So let's do that now.

Implementing the move functions

Even though moves in Undercut are just numbers from 1 to 10, humans and computers *determine* their moves in very different ways. Human players enter a number from 1 to 10 at the keyboard, while computer players use a function to generate their moves. Thus the Human and Computer classes need their own special-purpose get_move(self) methods.

Here is a get_move method for the human (the error messages have been shortened to save space; fuller and more user-friendly messages are given in the accompanying source code on the Web site):

```
class Human(Player):
    def __repr__(self):
        return 'Human(%s)' % str(self)

    def get_move(self):
        while True:
            try:
                n = int(input('%s move (1
                → - 10): ' % self.get_
                → name()))
                if 1 <= n <= 10:
                    return n
                else:
                    print('Oops!')
            except:
                print(Oops!')
```

This code asks the user to enter an integer from 1 to 10 and doesn't quit until the user does so. The try/except structure is used to catch the exception that the int function will throw if the user enters a non-integer (like "two").

For the computer's move, we will simply have it always return a random number from 1 to 10 (we can improve the computer strategy later if we want):

```
class Computer(Player):
    import random
    def __repr__(self):
        return 'Computer(%s)' % str(self)

    def get_move(self):
        return random.randint(1, 10)
```

Notice that we put `import random` inside the class definition. It is usually a good idea to put everything a class needs to work properly within the class itself.

Playing Undercut

With all the pieces in place, we can now start playing Undercut. Let's try a game between a human and a computer:

```
>>> c = Computer('Hal Bot')
>>> h = Human('Lia')
>>> play_undercut(c, h)
Lia move (1 - 10): 7
Hal Bot move: 10
Lia move: 7
(Computer(name = 'Hal Bot', score = 0),
→ Human(name = 'Lia', score = 0), 'draw:
→ no winner')
```

It's important to realize that the player objects must be created *outside* of the `play_undercut` function. That's good design: The `play_undercut` function worries only about playing the game, and not about how to initialize the player objects.

The `play_undercut` function returns a 3-tuple of the form (*p1*, *p2*, *message*). The *p1* and *p2* values are the player objects that were initially passed in; if one player happens to win the game, then her score will have been incremented. The *message* is a string indicating who won the game or if it was a draw.

Polymorphism in action

Now we will do something that is pretty remarkable when you think about it. Let's pass two computer players to play_undercut:

```
>>> c1 = Computer('Hal Bot')
>>> c2 = Computer('MCP Bot')
>>> play_undercut(c1, c2)
Hal Bot move: 8
MCP Bot move: 7
(Computer(name = 'Hal Bot', score = 0),
→ Computer(name = 'MCP Bot', score = 1),
→ 'MCP Bot wins!')
```

There's no human player in this game, so the user is not asked to enter a number.

We can also pass in two human players:

```
>>> h1 = Human('Bea')
>>> h2 = Human('Dee')
>>> play_undercut(h1, h2)
Bea move (1 - 10): 5
Dee move (1 - 10): 4
Bea move: 5
Dee move: 4
(Human(name = 'Bea', score = 0),
→ Human(name = 'Dee', score = 1),
→ 'Dee wins!')
```

Dumb Interface

While play_undercut works if you pass it two Human objects, it is not a very sensible interface: The second player will get to see the first player's move, and so need never lose the game. For this to actually be fun for two humans, you would need to think of some way to keep the first player's move hidden from the second player.

These two examples, plus the earlier one of a human playing against a computer, all show the power of *polymorphism*: We've used *the same* play_undercut function to get very different behaviors. Instead of writing three different functions, we only wrote one, and changed the objects we gave it.

In practice, this often turns out to be a big win. While it takes experience and careful attention to design details to make polymorphism work out, it is often worth the extra time and effort.

Learning More

This chapter introduced a few of the essentials of OOP. Python has many more OOP features you can learn about by reading the online documentation or by searching the Web for tutorials.

Creating good object-oriented designs is a major topic: Using objects *well* is much harder than merely *using* them. One popular methodology is *object-oriented design patterns*, which are proven recipes for using objects to solve common programming problems.

The most influential book on this topic is *Design Patterns: Elements of Reusable Object-Oriented Software*, by Erich Gamma, Richard Helm, Ralph Johnson, and John Vlissides. Once you've learned all the technical details of OOP, reading this book would be an excellent next step to learning about larger design issues.

POPULAR PYTHON PACKAGES

Part of the reason for Python's popularity is the availability of many high-quality libraries that help with various software tasks. In this appendix are descriptions of a few of the most popular packages.

It is useful to keep in mind that many of these packages may work only with specific versions of Python (which you can always download for free from www.python.org). In particular, many packages do not yet support Python 3, so you may need to use Python 2.6 (or later) to run some of these. Fortunately, if you already know Python 3, it is not too hard to step back a version to use Python 2. Appendix B briefly discusses some of the major differences between Python 2 and Python 3.

PIL: The Python Imaging Library

PIL (www.pythonware.com/products/pil) is an image-processing library. It works with many different kinds of image formats, and provides a number of useful image-processing functions for tasks such as cropping, resizing, rotation, and filtering.

Tkinter: Python GUIs

Tkinter comes with the Python library and is the standard means of accessing the popular Tk GUI tool kit. If you want to create a graphical user interface (GUI) in Python, this should be your first stop. See http://docs.python.org/dev/3.0/library/tkinter.html for more information.

Zope: A Web management system

Zope (www.zope.org) is a full-blown Web application server that you can use to host large and interactive Web sites. It is largely written in Python and uses Python as the main scripting language for creating new plug-ins. You can find lots of documentation for getting started on the Zope home page.

Django: Developing interactive Web sites

Django (www.djangoproject.com) is a framework for quickly creating interactive Web applications. Unlike Zope, it is not a complete Web server that works out of the box; rather, Django is a programming tool kit that makes it relatively easy to create new Web sites in a short time. In this way, it is similar to Ruby on Rails, but it uses Python instead of Ruby as the underlying programming language.

Pygame: 2D animation

Pygame (www.pygame.org) is a popular Python package that lets you create and control two-dimensional animations, especially for games. It provides tools for graphical animation, sound, and input devices such as joysticks. There are also introductory tutorials and sample programs at the pygame Web site to help get you started.

SciPy: Scientific computing

SciPy (www.scipy.org) is a large and popular library of software tools for scientific computing (it even has its own associated conferences!). It provides mathematical software to do things such as solve optimization problems, perform numerical linear algebra calculations, process signals, and much more.

Twisted: Network programming

Twisted (http://twistedmatrix.com/trac) is a popular Python library for network programming. It supports numerous networking protocols, and includes things like Web servers, mail servers, and chat clients/servers.

PyPI: The Python Package Index

The Python Package Index (http://pypi.python.org/pypi) is a frequently updated list of thousands of user-submitted Python packages. It's a good place to look for special-purpose Python libraries, or just to browse to see what uses Python has been put to.

You can easily find thousands of other Python packages by searching the Web: For almost any programming task that someone has done before, you are likely to find a Python library!

Comparing Python 2 and Python 3

Python 3 was released at the end of 2008 and marks a major update to Python. Some of the changes introduced in Python 3 break backward compatibility with earlier versions of Python, so to ease the transition for current Python developers, the development of Python 2 has continued in parallel with the newer Python 3.

In this chapter, we'll summarize some of the main changes to Python 3 and also explain how you can convert a Python 2 program to Python 3.

What's New in Python 3

Python 3 introduces many new features; the following are some of the most visible:

◆ Python 3's print function is indeed a function. In Python 2, print was a language construct, similar to if and for. The problem with Python 2's print was that it was difficult to modify—for example, changing print statements to print to a file instead of the console is much easier in Python 3 because you can just reassign the print function.

◆ Dividing integers in Python 3 works as you would expect when fractions are involved:

```
Python3>>> 1/2
0.5
```

However, Python 2 chops off all digits after the decimal when dividing integers:

```
Python2>>> 1/2
0
```

While Python 2's way of dividing integers appears in other programming languages, many programmers find it counterintuitive and the cause of subtle errors.

◆ Python 2 has two kinds of classes: *old-style classes* and *new-style classes*. Python 3 drops old-style classes completely.

◆ Python 3 renames a couple of important functions: The input and range functions are called raw_input and xrange in Python 2.

◆ The format strings described in Chapter 9 exist only in Python 3, and not Python 2. Python 2 only has string interpolation with the % operator.

Many other technical changes have been made in Python 3. For a complete list of differences, see "What's New in Python 3.0" (http://docs.python.org/dev/3.0/whatsnew/3.0.html).

Converting Python 2 to Python 3

Python developers have been quite aware of the difficulties of moving to a new version of Python, and so have provided a couple of tools to make the conversion easier.

The first tool is named 2to3 (http://docs. python.org/library/2to3.html), and is a program that does most of the work of converting Python 2 programs into equivalent Python 3 programs.

Another useful tool is Python 2, version 2.6 and above, which can provide warnings when you are using features that have changed in Python 3.

Which Version of Python Should You Use?

When deciding what version of Python to use—2 or 3—there are a few things to take into consideration:

◆ If you must work with programs that are written in Python 2, then it would make most sense to use to use Python 2 (2.6 or higher) and gradually move to Python 3.

◆ Some special-purpose libraries may only work with one version of Python, and so if you need to use one of those, your choice of Python may be constrained.

◆ If you are just starting out as a programmer, and have no old Python programs to maintain or special-purpose libraries that you must use, then Python 3 is probably the best choice.

INDEX

INDEX